Praie

Scott Kelso's new book, *Ice on Fire*, is a po... message relevant to to-day's world. It reminds us of the powerful spiritual heritage that is Methodism's, with great examples from John Wesley's life.

But this is not a book about the past. With prophetic perception, Scott analyzes the present situation of the church and its needs as well as what the church must become in order to meet the spiritual needs of the future. Scott is not some armchair theologian sitting in an ivory tower removed from the realities of life. Rather, he writes with the heart of a seasoned pastor with more than 30 years' experience listening to the heart cries of people. He writes from his own experience of the Spirit and invites, rather than condemns, the historic denominations and their people to join him and others who are experiencing a mighty move of God at this time.

Ice on Fire should not only be read by every Methodist; it should be read by all people who are hungry for more of God and how they could experience a visitation from God. This book will encourage the faith of all who read it, from the Pentecostals and Charismatics to the Methodists and Congregationalists, and all the other denominations and new independent churches and those in the new networks of the "post-denominational world" that is arising.

Not only do I heartily recommend the book, I recommend its author. Scott Kelso lives what he has written. He is a wonderful, well-trained pastor with a heart for the Peace of Jesus, the Power of the Spirit, and the Presence of the Father's embrace. *Ice on Fire* could be used by the Holy Spirit to warm the hearts of those who read it.

—*Randy Clark*
President of Global Awakening

❖❖❖

Scott Kelso's book on renewing the church has about it the ring of truth. The reason is that it comes out of the experience of a spiritually mature and successful pastor. He writes about what he has seen and experienced personally, which is in itself a remarkable story. Kelso is biblically grounded and impressively comprehensive in his personal reading. Thus, one encounters Stott, Packer, Guinness, Barna, McNutt, and Kraft—reflecting the best of both the evangelical and charismatic traditions. It's a powerful read and will be profitable to both clergy and laity. I heartily recommend it.

—*James V. Heidinger II*
President and Publisher
Good News: An Evangelical Renewal Movement within the United Methodist Church

---

In *Ice on Fire*, Scott Kelso shares the passion that kept him motivated as pastor of the same Methodist church for 30 years. Scott has been through many of the trials that today's pastors experience and has learned how to be a wise and successful leader. Through his faithful journey, he has discovered how the local church can be renewed. Scott is still on fire himself after 30 years, and in this inspiring book, he shares the secret of his fire with us.

—*Dr. Francis MacNutt*
Founder
Christian Healing Ministries, Inc.

The Lord says, "See, I am doing a new thing! Now it springs up: do you not perceive it?" (Is. 43:19). For years Scott Kelso has prayed and preached on the new thing God is doing. How well he has perceived it and now has written a long awaited book to underscore the principles and power of renewal. What a gift he has given to the church!

—*Rev. Terry Teykl*
Director
World Methodist Prayer Team

I've known Scott for most of his 33 years in ministry and have co-labored and served in leadership with him in many different settings. Because of our friendship and common vision for renewal of the church, I have also been related to the Trinity Church and have been privileged to preach there many times. The church is everything that Scott says it is!

Scott is a visionary leader with a passion for Christ and a heart of integrity who has much insight and wisdom to offer to the body of Christ. *Ice on Fire* will be an encouragement to any pastor or lay person who is experiencing renewal in their church or who is praying for renewal to begin. Even glaciers will melt when exposed to the fire of the Holy Spirit. This book, with the insights and stories that it offers, could be the catalyst for a fresh move of the Spirit in the lives and churches of those who read it!

—*Gary L. Moore*
Executive Director
Aldersgate Renewal Ministries

ICE ON FIRE

A New Day for the 21st Century Church

Scott Kelso

Nelson Books
A Division of Thomas Nelson Publishers
Since 1798

www.thomasnelson.com

Published in Nashville, Tennessee, by Thomas Nelson, Inc.
www.thomasnelson.com

Nelson Books titles may be purchased in bulk for educational, business,
fundraising, or sales promotional use. For information, please email
SpecialMarkets@ThomasNelson.com.

Unless otherwise stated, all Scripture passages are from the Holy Bible, New
International Version® (NIV) copyright © 1973, 1978, 1984 by International
Bible Society. Used by permission of Zondervan Publishing House. All rights
reserved.

Other Scripture references are from the following sources: The King James
Version of the Bible (KJV). The Revised Standard Version of the Bible (rsv),
copyright © National Council of Churches of Christ in America.

Ice on Fire

ISBN: 0-8499-1874-X

Printed in the United States of America
1 2 3 4 5 6 — 09 08 07 06

Dedication

I dedicate this book to the memory of Dr. Lon R. Woodrum, poet, author, and evangelist in the United Methodist Church. Lon was also my mentor and friend of the long gospel road. His heart encouraged me to excel in the ministry of the local church, having often been prophetic beyond my wildest dreams. He is greatly missed, but his memory endures.

Contents

Foreword

Vinson Synan

I have known Scott Kelso for many years as a wonderful brother in Christ. We have worked together in many meetings planning renewal conferences and promoting charismatic renewal in the churches. I have also preached in his great United Methodist Church in Pickerington, Ohio, where I have seen the mighty work that God has raised up under his ministry. I have found Scott to be a man of great integrity and spiritual insight with a passion for the renewing work of the Holy Spirit. During these years I have seen him grow in stature and respect as a leader of leaders.

Born in Dayton, Ohio, in 1948, Kelso was converted to Christ as a freshman in college in 1969. That year he also married his wife, Linda Mae, who presented him with three children, Daniel, Noelle, and Alain. In 1970, his life was forever changed when he received the Baptism in the Holy Spirit in a Catholic convent in Dayton. After earning the B.A. degree at Ohio State University in 1970, he earned the Master of Divinity degree from the United Theological Seminary in Dayton, Ohio in 1973. In that same year he also became pastor of the Trinity United Methodist Church in Pickerington where he has served for thirty-two years. During this time he constructed a sanctuary seating 1,000 and built one of the strongest United Methodist churches in Ohio.

His influence as a loyal son of the United Methodist Church has made him a leading voice for renewal in his own church. He has served as a delegate to three General Conferences of the United Methodist Church (1996, 2000, and 2004) where his voice has been raised in the cause of biblical values and spiritual renewal. He is one of the shining examples of a mainline pastor who brought charismatic renewal to his congregation and who remained widely respected in his denomination. Along the way, he served from 1997 to 2001 as President of Aldersgate Renewal Ministries (ARM), the voice of charismatic renewal in the United Methodist Church.

Kelso has also served as a national leader for renewal. For many years he represented Methodists in the North American Renewal Service Committee (NARSC), a group that conducted several massive charismatic congresses. His most recent leadership role in the renewal is as Secretary of the Charismatic Leaders Fellowship, a spiritual think-tank with members from many denominations. He has served in this capacity since 2002.

Beyond this, he has grown to be a very important leader of pastors of many churches in the greater Columbus, Ohio area. For several years he has led the Capital City Association of Ministries and Churches. This group numbers no less than 200 churches.

In this book, *Ice on Fire: A New Day for the 21st Century Church,* Kelso writes from a rich background of pastoral care, having served for thirty-two years as pastor of the same congregation. When reading this book, one feels the fire that burns in his bones. In *Ice on Fire*, Kelso draws from biblical sources for much of his teaching. He also displays a fine sense of history as he writes about renewal all the way from John Wesley to John Wimber. Perhaps the most arresting parts of the book are his sharing of his own experiences as a pastor. One might say that he writes from the trenches on the front lines of the spiritual battles of recent times.

In the end, Kelso is optimistic about the prospects of renewal in the churches. His sections on the Holy Spirit and charismatic renewal are prophetic statements about the direction of the church in the 21st century. I pray that many pastors as well as laypersons will read this book and will be changed from coldness and ice to firebrands for God.

Vinson Synan
Dean of the School of Divinity
Regent University
Virginia Beach, Virginia

Acknowledgments

I first want to thank Mrs. Beverly Garrison for her long hours typing the manuscript and her helpful administrative skills. Years ago Bev told me that she would type the manuscript, in the event that I would write one. Thank you so much.

In addition, I wish to thank June Allen and Ginger Richards for their very helpful contribution in editorial changes. Their input was most valuable. I also want to thank Gary Moore, the executive director of Aldersgate Renewal Ministries and my longtime friend in the Lord, for his help in writing chapter four of this book. The ministry of ARM has been an important influence in my journey. Thank you to Vinson Synan who encouraged me at many points to write this book. His valuable counsel as to format and process has been greatly appreciated.

A huge hug and thank you to the saints at Trinity Church in Pickerington, Ohio for their faith, patience, and love in giving me three months off to write this book and for providing a lifetime laboratory where I could grow and bloom as a pastor.

And finally, to my wife, Linda, who has always been at my side and believed in me every step of the way, I say thank you and I love you. Together, we have experienced the goodness of God and look forward to the future in serving Christ to the close of the day.

ICE ON FIRE

A NEW DAY FOR THE 21ST CENTURY CHURCH

Introduction

People long to be a part of something great! During thirty-six weeks, beginning in February each year, hundreds of thousands of people jam motor speedways to watch their favorite NASCAR driver compete for the crown. Last fall, over one hundred thousand people assembled in cities across the United States in hopes of eventually becoming the next "American Idol." Only one will be chosen. Each Sunday, millions of people attend church services across our nation, not realizing they are part of the greatest people movement in history—an unbroken chain of worshippers known as the Christian church.

Unlike NASCAR or *American Idol*, in the church everyone wins because the one who has preceded us, Jesus Christ, is both a winner and is great. He is presiding over the greatest religious expression in history: the Christian faith. Christianity is more than showing up for the rehearsal (Sunday church) or crossing the finish line (taking your last breath). All who purposely give their lives to Jesus Christ are destined for greatness in the kingdom of God—in this life and in the life to come.

My heart longs to see manifest what I believe God has carried in His heart from the beginning of time—a church here on earth that adequately reflects His wonderful story of redemption. A church that is so caught up in His greatness, so infused by His power—a church so motivated by His love that she burns hot for Him. Yes, a church on fire! This book is about the "Fire Church" coming into her 21st century destiny.

In some ways this volume is prescriptive for pastors and leaders across the nation who realize that the North American church is due for some radical change. As pastors and leaders, you passion-

1

ately love God and are concerned over the state of the church in America. Further, you know there is more, but how much more and what kind of more?

In other ways this volume is reflective of current war stories and beachheads that have been secured on the plain of church renewal. Churches are coming alive to a new day in God. Many of these churches can be seen as a kind of "forerunner spirit" for what God is about to do en masse across America. People who have studied the history of revivals like Michael L. Brown, C. Peter Wagner, and Tommy Tenney believe we are on the precipice of one of the greatest outpourings in history. Young people from New York to Los Angeles are being positioned to become a mighty force for God. We are in a day when God is not nearly as interested in the name over the door as He is in what is happening inside the house.

I boast of no special revelation as I write this treatise. I am a pastor in a local denominational church with my own mix of personality flaws and ineptitude. However, I have carried a passionate desire in ministry to know God through His Word and Spirit. What I bring to the table is a willing and open heart before the Lord. Whatever God wants to do is okay by me. If there is anything God can use in me, then I say, "Have at it!"

One of the central dynamics of my ministry over the last thirty-two years has been to attempt to create an atmosphere where the presence of God is welcome. In most of the contemporary church models today (the cell-based model, the program-based model, the purpose-driven model, the apostolic model, the seeker model, and the blended model), the emphasis is to attract more people to the church. I believe, however, the great need today is to attract more of God to our churches. When we make room for God, the people will come. The New Testament verifies this fact.

Read the first ten chapters of the Gospel of Mark. Wherever Jesus went, there was standing room only. On one occasion, they tore off the roof of the home while He was speaking, in order to lower a sick person down into the presence of God. For further examples, read the progression in the Book of Acts, beginning with three thousand people saved on the day of Pentecost (Acts 2:41, 47; 4:4; 5:14; 6:7; 8:12; 9:31).

I have also found that when the presence of God comes, everything is negotiable—even the Sunday morning schedule. There have been total strangers attending our worship service on Sunday mornings when the Spirit of God breaks in upon us. This is when a pastor really prays, "Lord, don't let anything crazy happen." Many times, in this kind of atmosphere, I do not get to preach. God takes us a different direction.

Being swept into the "jet stream" of God's Spirit, unusual things can take place: spontaneous healings, testimonies, prophetic words, and more. Amazingly, in the vast majority of these experiences when we have been apprehended by His presence, our visitors are not offended. Quite to the contrary, they are curious and say, "Are you sure this is a Methodist church?" My reply is, "It is indeed a Methodist church, and one that John Wesley would be proud of, I might add."

Speaking of Wesley, there was a time in his ministry when he allowed God to carry him by the wings of the Spirit into a new day. I speak of none other than his inauguration to "field preaching." Here is how it happened. John Wesley had a definite conversion experience on May 24, 1738.

> In the evening I went very unwillingly to a society on Aldersgate Street, where one was reading Luther's preface to the Epistle to the Romans. About a quarter before nine, while he was describing the change which God works in the heart through faith in Christ, I felt my heart strangely warmed. I felt I did trust in Christ, Christ alone for salvation; And an assurance was given me, that he had taken away my sins, even mine, and saved me from the law of sin and death.[1]

This became a huge turnaround in Wesley's life. Things really began to "pop" for Wesley following this event. However, approximately nine months later, a second event transpired that radically altered John Wesley's life until his last breath. George Whitfield,

Wesley's close evangelist friend, wrote him a letter, requesting that John come to Bristol, England, to help him.[2]

The key here is that Whitfield was an open-air preacher, and Wesley was a refined Oxford don, used to preaching in church buildings. John's brother, Charles, was not in favor of this invitation by Whitfield; neither was the Methodist Society. The journal records: "My brother Charles would scarce bear the mention of it."[3] Finally, following an extended discussion, "We at length all agreed to decide it by lot. And by this it was determined I should go."[4] I find this very stimulating. Here was the greatest religious figure of the 18th century, minding his own business in his religious tradition, and God came along and said, "You know something, John? I have something new for you." It was field preaching. This did not come naturally for Wesley. Listen to his firsthand account:

> I could scarce reconcile myself at first to this strange way of preaching in the fields, of which he set me an example on Sunday; having been all my life (until very lately) so tenacious of every point relating to decency and order, that I should have thought the saving of souls almost a sin, if it had not been done in a church.[5]

Just a few days later, this entry: "At four in the afternoon, I submitted to be more vile, and proclaimed in the highways the glad tidings of salvation, speaking from a little eminence in a ground adjoining to the city, to about three thousand people."[6]

The moral of this lesson is: Don't check out before God's purpose is accomplished in you. It may involve "unfamiliar territory," but God will get you to the appointed destination. Let's remember, friends, this business of church is not a mechanical, pre-rehearsed regimen that we blindly follow, hoping that God is watching. No, this thing called ministry is supernatural, dynamic, and Spirit-generated. We are meant to thrive under the leading and direction of a supernatural God. We have to be willing for God to apprehend us—one ear to heaven, the other to earth, hearing what God is saying and then acting in obedience. This is what makes church so exciting.

In my early years of ministry, I knew just enough to be dangerous. Thirty years later, I suppose I am still dangerous, but now what I know, I really know. There are some powerful principles in the Word of God that can fuel every church in America. God is just waiting to light the fire.

You are about to read a book on what God has shown me in the press of Christian ministry. I started out in a small, country evangelical church that was typical of a majority of churches in 1974. The members were good "salt of the earth" people who paid their bills, served their communities in various capacities, and faithfully attended church on Sunday. However, there was nothing present that was representative of the church in the Book of Acts. I suppose I could have "paid the rent," as we say in church-growth circles, and had a fine professional career in ministry. But my heart's desire was not to go the route of the professional matrix. I wanted more.

I yearned to experience an apostolic ministry. After all, John Wesley experienced it, and it is our heritage in United Methodism. Early in my ministry, the Spirit of God was whispering to me, "Come follow me; I will take you as far as you want to go." And off I went—sometimes bewildered, sometimes perplexed, but always with a sense of adventure. I would ask, "Oh God, what great things are we going to do together today?"

I have always said to myself that I never want to come to the end of my ministry, then look back and lament, "I wish I had done it differently." I can truly say, for the most part, I would not have done anything differently. God has been faithful, and I want to proclaim it!

You see, almost every pastor in the beginning makes a strategic choice as to what style of ministry he or she will assume. For me, it was all about God and the Bible. Either I was going to experience what I read in the Bible, or I would pump gas or hang drywall. I was determined not to play games with God. It always perplexed me why we become so selective in terms of the Bible. Ministry leaders would be appalled to be cheated out of the love, hope, and peace promised to every believer in the New Testament. They preach it, and they expect it. So why do we casually forget about the miracles, the healings, the signs and wonders? Are these not available to us as well? The Bible has come down to us as a complete story. Why not receive it completely?

I have also found that a great motivator in ministry is desperation. Three months into our present assignment, my wife Linda and I knelt down in the parsonage one day and prayed, "Lord, if you don't help us, we are finished." We had encountered enough of the "natural" in people to know we needed the "supernatural" to survive. Lo and behold, God showed up and, as they say, the rest is history.

We are facing a situation today in the church where the frustration level in ministry is very high. Such things as long hours, low pay, high debt load, unrealistic expectations, and living in a "fishbowl" are taking their toll. When you add to these the unbiblical cultural expectation that the pastor is trained to do the ministry while the people sit back and watch the shepherd perform, it's not a pretty picture.

In this context, pastors pastor and congregations congregate. And the beat goes on. Someone said, "The pastor is paid to be good, and the rest of us are just good for nothing." Meanwhile, the morale of clergy is plummeting greatly. In addition, shepherding the flock has degenerated into policing the troops. This is verified by statistics (see Chapter 9). I know this is hard to believe, but this is where we are in America today.

Far too many pastors spend much of the time in ministry putting out fires or in crisis-mode management. In such an atmosphere, morale takes a direct hit. Creativity is stifled. Worst of all, God is not glorified. How can we expect others to come to a living faith in our churches, when just beneath the surface there is chaos and confusion? Too many leaders live their lives in "silent desperation."

One of my dear members, Robert Lewis, before he recently passed away, recounted a true story to me. Bob had a way of conveying a story that left a lasting impression. It seems that Bob had an Aunt Mabel who lived in Elwood City, Pennsylvania, who was greatly overweight. One day she walked to the outhouse to "take care of business." While there, the unthinkable happened—she fell through! Finding herself hopelessly stuck in the "grimpen mire" (Sherlock Holmes in *The Hound of the Baskervilles*), the only way out was to be rescued; and rescued she was—by the local fire department. The first thing she said to her would-be rescuers was, and I quote, "Just shoot me." Hurriedly, the firemen had to assemble a block and tackle mechanism to hoist her out of the dastardly pit.

There are many pastors across America stuck in dysfunctional churches, and they are saying silently in their hearts, "Just shoot me." These pastors are highly trained, well motivated, and have responded to the call of God on their lives; but something is desperately wrong in "pewland." Ministry is not going well, and they see little hope in sight. I regularly receive calls from pastors all across the nation who are stuck in the ministry context. They are frustrated, angry, and many are at their wits' end. I have ministered to some who are suicidal. The current dropout rate for clergy verifies this disconcerting lament.

This book is an attempt not only to diagnose some of the problems in the American church, but also to provide hope for the many servant leaders marooned on the island of discontent and running out of food. God is in the rescuing business, and the darkest hour is just before dawn. The following pages are not intended to suggest a quick fix, or "three steps to parish bliss." The world does not work that way. However, I am prepared to declare that "the Spirit of Him who raised Jesus from the dead dwells in you" (Romans 8:11), and the church is His—not ours.

A combination of prayer (including spiritual warfare), joined to the Word of God, the Almighty, still "gives life to the dead and calls things that are not as though they were" (Romans 4:17). He still is the God of the miraculous and stands firmly behind His ageless Word that nothing shall separate us from the love of God in Christ Jesus our Lord (see Romans 8:39).

Finally, I urge all readers of this book to do so with an open mind, prayerfully, and hopefully with people in your leadership circle. I regularly review books with my staff. Read it with your parish council, a Sunday school class, or your trusted prayer warriors. Let the Holy Spirit guide you. This book can provide a platform for useful discussion, without you personally having to be the focal point.

The truth is, scores of churches across the United States are coming alive, even to the point of fire. God is again breathing on the church in this hour. Your church can be one of those churches. If you are going from "Ice to Fire," you are going in the right direction. Stay focused and remember, "For the eyes of the LORD range throughout the earth to strengthen those whose hearts are fully committed to him" (2 Chronicles 16:9).

Chapter 1

The God Who Answers by Fire

The cool mist from the elevation wrapped itself around the top of the mountain. The mountain was Mt. Carmel, a famous peak along a "string of mountains that run about 15 miles through central Palestine and jut into the Mediterranean Sea."[7] The year was 871 B.C. The occasion was one of the classic confrontations in all of the Bible between light and darkness.

The prophet Elijah remains one of the great personalities of the Old Testament period. He was a colorful figure, having been used by God to perform eye-opening miracles at a time of national crisis. The struggle between the forces of Baal and the worship of Jehovah was very real, with far-reaching implications for the nation. Furthermore, the entire prophetic movement was born to parallel the kingdom period of the Old Testament. The prophets were advisors to the kings.

The idea of kingship in Israel was not generated by Jehovah but was adapted as a practice similar to the surrounding nations at the time (1 Samuel 8:19). It was what the people wanted, and God gave them their king. God also provided for the "mouthpiece"—the prophet to help the king discern (judge between the clean and the unclean) Israel's devotion to Jehovah.

The prophets—beginning with Samuel (1 Samuel 3:20; 9:9) all the way through Malachi—had their hands full. Many of the kings of Israel were found doing their own thing, while the national reputation and the covenant with Jehovah were placed in jeopardy. During Elijah's watch, Ahab was one of the worst.

Ahab was the son of the man who had built Samaria, Omri, the greatest king of the Northern Kingdom, historically speaking. The historical annals of the kings of Assyria for a hundred years after his day spoke about the Northern Kingdom as "the house of Omri."[8]

Unfortunately, Omri was not devoted to Jehovah and led the nation down the path of sin and rebellion. His son, Ahab, furthered the downward slide. Three "great sins" plagued Israel through its history, and Ahab excelled in all of them. They were: breaking the Sabbath, intermarrying, and idol worshipping (spiritual adultery).

The Lord God Maintains His Witness

By the time Elijah comes on the scene, Israel's "faithfulness index" was pretty grim.

> Ahab son of Omri did more evil in the eyes of the LORD than any of those before him. He not only considered it trivial to commit the sins of Jeroboam son of Nebat, but he also married Jezebel, daughter of Ethbaal king of the Sidonians, and began to serve Baal and worship him. He set up an altar for Baal in the temple of Baal that he built in Samaria. Ahab also made an Asherah pole and did more to provoke the LORD, the God of Israel, to anger than did all the kings of Israel before him (1 Kings 16:30–33).

When we understand that the worship of Baal was performed by a fertility cult and the worship involved sexual immorality as a religious act, we can understand the grave concern, especially in the heart of a prophet. Ahab's alliance with Jezebel seals the fate. Jezebel wanted to literally erase the name of Jehovah and His worship from the face of the earth and to erect in its place Baal worship as the official expression of worship for the Northern Kingdom. These were dark days indeed.

Into the fray steps Elijah, who proposes a kind of contest between his God, Jehovah, and the unauthorized god, Baal. Ahab took the bait, and they met on Mt. Carmel. Four hundred and fifty prophets of Baal went against Elijah and the living God. "How long will you waver between two opinions? If the LORD is God, follow him; but if Baal is God, follow him" (1 Kings 18:21).

One can almost feel the tension building. The prophets of Baal were to choose for themselves a bull, cut it in pieces, and lay it on the wood, but put no fire to it. "Then you call on the name of your god, and I will call on the name of the LORD. The god who answers by fire—he is God" (1 Kings 18:24).

The prophets of Baal cried to their god all day long to no avail. There was no fire. Elijah mocked them, heightening the tension. Still no fire. Finally, they began to cut themselves, raving around with blood gushing out; still no fire.

By the time of the evening oblation, it was Elijah's turn. He prepared his altar in the same manner, requesting scrutiny, so there would be no misunderstanding. He built an altar with twelve stones, representing the twelve tribes of Israel. He dug a trench around his altar and filled it with water, soaking the wood, the dead animal, and all the adjacent ground. Finally, it was Elijah's turn to pray.

> At the time of sacrifice, the prophet Elijah stepped forward and prayed: "O LORD, God of Abraham, Isaac and Israel, let it be known today that you are God in Israel and that I am your servant and have done all these things at your command. Answer me, O LORD, answer me, so these people will know that you, O LORD, are God, and that you are turning their hearts back again." Then the fire of the LORD fell and burned up the sacrifice, the wood, the stones and the soil, and also licked up the water in the trench (1 Kings 18:36–38).

Elijah had the false prophets seized, taken down to the brook Kishon, and killed. The name of Jehovah was vindicated.

God Still Answers by Fire

My thesis is that God is still answering by fire, and His famed name is still alive in the earth. Something very dramatic happened on Mt. Carmel over three thousand years ago. It is a breathtaking view overlooking the Valley of Jezreel and the Plain of Esdraelon. It was there that the whole nation of Israel saw God burn water. For our enlightenment-prone brothers and sisters, He probably split the water into H_2 and O before igniting the gases. This process is known as disassociation. After all, is there anything too difficult for God (see Jeremiah 32:17)?

The God whom we worship today is still answering by fire. He is the true and living God, and He desires that we burn hot for Him. Jesus said, "I have come to bring fire on the earth, and how I wish it were already kindled! But I have a baptism to undergo, and how distressed I am until it is completed" (Luke 12:49–50).

God's people have been crying out for most of the 20th century for Him to answer by fire. The world culture has presented us with a great challenge—similar to Elijah's. It desires our devotion to its idols and its practices. Our God says, "I will have no other gods before me" (see Jonah 2:8).

I believe the hour is upon us as Christians to walk in the power of His anointing and to witness to a dying culture. God is anointing His church with fire, and it is transferable. It will be like Peter's shadow or Paul's handkerchief. Nothing will ever be more important than hearing His voice and obeying—not your house, your car, your children, your family, your hobbies . . . nothing.

God's plan is a good plan for your life. He will not give you something that will spoil your fun or ruin your life. That is the agenda of the devil. God does want to ruin us for the ordinary; but what is so great about the ordinary? I believe the Lord is telling those reading this book to go ahead and jump into the deep end.

One thing I have learned in ministry over the last 30 years is that there is always more in God. We never really arrive. However, I have met some people who thought they had arrived. That discussion is for another time.

I was ministering in the city of Cabanatuan in the Philippines in January of 2001. My partner and I had been dispatched to the Wesley University for an all-day rally with the student body. First we met privately with the staff. We laid hands on them and prayed that the holiness movement Wesley spawned would come upon the student body. I thought to myself, how different this ministry is from that in the United States—they are so receptive, and we are so guarded.

When we arrived at the school coliseum a bit later, it was jammed with young people. At least eight hundred to a thousand people waited for ministry. After tag-team preaching, which lasted all day, we actually saw almost the entire assembly receive Christ as Savior and receive the Baptism in the Holy Spirit with fire. The people turned out en masse, with little or no coercion, and were ready to worship and receive from the Word of God. It was an amazing day.

Fuel and Fire

It is going to take fire to win the post-modern generation—fire and the supernatural. There are three things required to make fire: fuel, oxygen, and combustion. I believe we are the fuel, the Word of God is the oxygen (the atmosphere to live), and the Holy Spirit is the combustion. I realize it is a formative theme in the Scriptures. Note how many of the following verses either refer to cleansing, purification, or judgment.

> Leviticus 6:12a—"The fire on the altar must be kept burning, it must not go out."
>
> Exodus 3:2—The bush burned with fire but was not consumed.
>
> 2 Kings 2:11—Elijah was swept away in a chariot of fire.
>
> Isaiah 30:27—His tongue was a consuming fire.
>
> Jeremiah 23:29—God's Word is like fire.
>
> Zechariah 3:2—"Is not this man a burning stick snatched from the fire?"
>
> Malachi 3:2—"He will be like a refiner's fire."

Matthew 3:11b—"He will baptize you with the Holy Spirit
and with fire."

Luke 12:49—"I have come to bring fire on the earth and
how I wish it were already kindled."

Acts 2:3—". . . tongues of fire that separated and came to
rest on each of them."

1 Corinthians 3:13b—A man's works will be revealed by
fire.

1 Thessalonians 5:19—"Do not put out the Spirit's fire."

Hebrews 12:29—"For our God is a consuming fire."

The fact is that God did not come to pamper our dysfunction,
but to change us radically. Few things are as lethal as fire. As the fire
of God purifies, it burns out the sin and causes a desire for the
things of God—a hunger for holiness. This Baptism of Fire is carrying the church worldwide into the 21st century.

According to recent projections, there are 625 million Spirit-
baptized Christians in the world today. That is the largest single
section of the Christian church, other than the Roman Catholic
Church. Believe it or not, 116 million of those are Roman
Catholics.[9]

Religion in America has, for too long, been a kind of hobby. We
squeeze it in along with everything else we have to do, but the
winds of God are bringing change. Formerly nominal churches are
catching the wind of the Spirit and taking new territory. Missions,
evangelism, signs, and wonders are on the rise in unexpected
places. In the United Methodist Church, local congregations are
catching the fire all across the country. A ring of Wesley is in the air,
and no one is quite sure where it will peak.

Harvey Cox, Professor of Religion at Harvard University, has
noted the turning to God in our culture.

Nearly three decades ago I wrote a book, *The Secular City*,
in which I tried to work out a theology for the 'post religious' age that many sociologists had confidently assured us
was coming. Since then, however, religion—or at least some

religions—seem to have gained a new lease on life. Today it is secularity, not spirituality, which may be headed for extinction.[10]

In addition, the center of gravity for Christianity has shifted from the Western world to Asia, Africa, and South America. These areas of the world are generally poor, more conservative theologically, embracing clear moral boundaries in living, and very strong in the supernatural. Western Christianity will learn to recognize what God is doing in the world and hopefully "move with the cloud" because our God is on the move.

The Experience at Washington Crossing

One of the churches that has been impacted by the fire of God is Washington Crossing United Methodist Church outside Philadelphia, Pennsylvania. Read the firsthand testimony of its pastor, Scott McDermott, relating how the Spirit fell on a Sunday morning in 1994. Perhaps you can identify with his inner struggle to allow God to have His way.

As I look at Washington Crossing United Methodist Church, I can scarcely believe it is the same congregation I came to years ago. Worship is alive and vibrant; some even dance in celebration. People are frequently so moved by God's power that they prostrate themselves before the Lord at the close of the service. Our prayer ministries continue to multiply and expand, and our Sunday night prayer service continues to draw people from our congregation and around the region to call upon God. At times, it is red hot in fervent prayer as the Spirit empowers and guides us in our intercession. Yet this is only the starting place for effective ministry and mission. God brings us into the fire of His presence, and then sends us out to the world. Teams regularly going from the Crossing into the inner city, reaching out across cross-cultural challenges and divides, and teams heading around the world, ranging from the Arctic Circle to Cuba; God has been sending us with His heart, with His passion, and renewed strength. I marvel when I think about it really. How did we get here?

It all began in July of 1994 on an ordinary Sunday morning. I was preaching through the Book of Nehemiah that Sunday. My topic was the Feast of Tabernacles, a time of Jewish celebration filled with seven days of praise. Understand the comment I was about to make in my message was only rhetorical in nature, and my intention was only to bring a little levity into my sermon. What did I say? I simply said, "What would happen if we declared seven days of rejoicing here at the Crossing?" A well-respected and reserved member of our congregation sitting in the back of the church surprisingly responded in a loud voice, "Let's do it." His comment startled everyone, including me. In those days it was hard to get an "Amen," let alone a "Let's do it" comment from the congregation. I have since concluded that when parishioners begin speaking such words of faith from the back row of a Methodist church, God may be up to something.

In our Sunday night service, there seemed to be new and inexplicable enthusiasm. The singing seemed livelier than normal, and I think we may have even clapped our hands to the beat of the music that night. Somewhere in the middle of the singing, I felt compelled to announce, "Tonight begins seven nights of praise." When I did, the people seemed to erupt in excitement over the announcement. Still, it begged the question, just what would we do for seven nights? I was not the only one to see the problem. My worship leader came over to me at the close of the service and asked, "Scott, what will we do for seven nights?" I said, "I don't know. I have never done this before. Give me a hymnal and I'll figure it out."

The next day I planned a perfectly timed one-hour service. I divided the service into six ten-minute segments, assigning different areas of emphasis to each section: praise, thanksgiving, confession of sins, personal prayer for ourselves, silent prayer for others, and then the grand finale—ten good minutes of nonstop praise. The first night hardly drew a large crowd. Perhaps twenty came, and we executed the game plan to perfection. The only problem was, at the end of the evening I felt the Spirit say to me, "Scott, this is fine, but tomorrow night I want to invite the people forward and I want you to anoint them with oil and pray a Spirit of joy over their lives." Now, that may sound good to you, but it didn't to me. In fact, I had taught against doing such overt charismatic acts in a non-charismatic setting. I had even taught a workshop in which I strongly advised against what I was about to do. You can imagine my internal angst over this.

The next night about twenty people came again to the meeting. We walked through the same orderly process of worship, only this time at 8:00 p.m. I decided to call people forward in a prayer line to anoint them with oil and pray a Spirit of joy over each life. I instructed my worship leader to play hymns and choruses as I prayed for the people. Reluctantly each person came forward. I anointed the first person, then the second, but by the time I got to the third person, they were so overcome with the Spirit that they collapsed to the floor. Then the next in line fell to the ground as I prayed for them. Soon men began rushing up to the front of the church to catch the people as they dropped suddenly under the power of God.

In the midst of my praying for people, I realized the music had stopped. I turned to look for my worship leader, but he was nowhere to be found. My first thought was that he left the building in protest to what was happening. My worship leader—himself an ordained United Methodist pastor—and I had never discussed such manifestations of the Spirit. To my surprise, he had not left the building. Instead, he was standing in line awaiting prayer. Soon he stood in front of me, arms folded across his chest, with his head down as he approached me. I never touched him. I never touched him. All I said was, "Receive the mantle of David." At those words, he fell to the ground in a heap, telling me later that he was thinking as he was falling, "But God, I don't do this."

The next night 125 people came to our service. Yes, we walked through the same order of service for one hour, and then I began to pray. People stood in a prayer line for hours, waiting for me to pray for them. Words of knowledge were vivid and clear. The anointing was powerful and amazing. It was about 10:00 that night. I had now prayed two hours nonstop for people, and still they filled the aisle of the church, awaiting prayer. To my left a dance circle had begun to form to celebrate the visitation of God. As I looked out into our lobby I saw another dance circle had formed. A cloud seemed to hover over the room. I remember stepping back, looking up and saying to God, "What is going on?" God was inviting us to step into His fire. Each night for the entire week, the same scene was repeated.

I must confess, I did not know in those days where it was all going. But perhaps when one walks with God, one never truly knows. All you ever know is that wherever you go, you don't want to go without Him. And that is how we still feel at the Crossing. That week in July 1994, was the beginning of the journey to where we are today—a church hungry for God, desperate for more of His presence, and eager to be used of Him, no matter what the cost.[11]

It's Time to Grow Up

I believe God wants the church to grow into a fuller New Testament expression. In John 14:6–19 and 16:7, Jesus was preparing His disciples for His departure. Jesus was not talking about leaving them in terms of severing the relationship, but about a progression of that relationship into a more rewarding dimension. This is exactly what happened at Washington Crossing Church.

It is interesting to me that after Jesus ascended to the Father and sent the Holy Spirit upon the church, one never hears the disciples "hankering for the good old days" when Jesus was among them. No. They were fellowshipping with Him on a whole new level. They were walking in the Spirit and were quite content.

Think of it this way. As people grow and mature, they leave childhood behind. Being absorbed into adulthood, they have naturally moved on physically, emotionally, and intellectually. For them to revert to childhood would be wholly unproductive. Similarly, the disciples progressed from a relationship with Jesus as a human person to the greater reality of a relationship with Jesus as a Spirit person. This progression is a part of the design of God.

John 4:24 says, "God is Spirit, and his worshipers must worship in Spirit and in truth." It took Jesus in the flesh to get us there. That is why Paul says in 2 Corinthians 5:16 (RSV), "Even though we once regarded Christ from a human point of view, we regard him thus no longer."

First Corinthians 15:45 says that through His death and resurrection, Jesus became a "life-giving spirit." This is not common sense covered in spiritual coating, nor is it living by spiritual principles alone. No, this is a dynamic, living, daily-informed walk of the Holy Spirit in partnership with Him. This is where the church is headed as we move into the future.

This is not common sense covered in spiritual coating, nor is it living by spiritual principles alone. No, this is a living, dynamic, daily-informed walk of the Holy Spirit in partnership with Him. This is where the church is headed as we move into the future.

A few years ago I asked my congregation these questions:

- Can God speak to you any way He wants?
- Can God tell you anything He wants?
- Can God use you for any purpose He wants?

These are far-reaching questions, yet they serve as conditions that the Holy One is offering to our generation, if we are to be used in these days. If we are to leave a mark on the world, then we must begin to dream and live in a lifestyle that expects God to manifest. Otherwise, the Bible will just be ancient history and will not really impact our lives.

We must realize that most of the personalities in the Bible were ordinary people like you and me who were swept into an extraordinary God. God is always looking for us in the midst of the ordinary and menial things of life, and there He causes history to be written. Consider these:

- Delivering lunch to the troops—David
- Holding a rope and lowering someone in a basket—Paul
- Hanging a scarlet cord in the window—Rahab
- Climbing a tree to see Jesus—Zaccheus
- Going to the house of a stranger and not knowing why—Peter
- Giving your last few cents—The widow
- Giving your most important possession—Mary

All these people and more have been memorialized in the record of God's history because they were only doing menial things at the moment. In the midst of it, they became the gears upon which history was made. The question is, will we be those persons? Will I be that pastor, and will our church be the church to make waves for the Almighty?

Getting Personal

What the traditional denominational church has done for too long is, on the one hand, looked at the culture, and on the other hand, looked at the Word of God; then she set her standards somewhere in between. This in turn leads to what I call "generational slide," where each generation loses more and more moral ground. Should we be surprised that presidents commit adultery in the Oval Office, and corporations fudge the books to avert stockholder accountability?

What we really need to recognize is our bankruptcy before God and our need for God to visit our churches and our lives. The plain fact is the church of our generation has failed to infect the culture with Christianity. We have many trappings of the faith, but we lack the New Testament power—the salt and light to change the culture. We can never get to where we need to go if we first don't recognize where we are! To deny this truth is to stick our heads in the sand and play make-believe.

No amount of escapism or positive thinking will turn this ship around. In our complacency we are like those on the Titanic, thinking there is no way this ship could go down. How wrong they were, and how wrong we are as well.

We have a defective church because we have a defective gospel. It has become a mixture—what the missionaries call "syncretism." With it we have produced a church with spiritual defects. We do not call people to renounce and forsake everything for the gospel. If we did, we would see a higher level of discipleship in the American church. After all, Jesus is called Savior some twenty times in the New Testament, and Lord some two hundred times.

Holiness is not an option. It is the life that God has for us. We are all going to have to "get down and get real" to recover a sense of direction. There are emerging signs of hope. For example, a pastor sparked an awakening in a Texas church a few years ago with a simple act of obedience.

A Texas pastor's shocking act of humility has ushered in a powerful move of God at his church. Members of Promised Land Church in Austin were stunned when Kenneth Phillips preached about the need to root out pride—and suddenly removed the hairpiece he had worn for more than twenty years. "People were absolutely shocked, and then they began to fall on their faces on the floor," said Phillips' son Randy, an associate minister at the two thousand-strong independent Pentecostal church. "Ever since then it has been the deepest, most intense worship we have ever known. God has completely turned this place upside down."

The church has had to add a second Sunday morning service to cope with the increased attendance. More than two hundred people have been baptized, and many others baptized in the Holy Spirit. There have been reports of healings, and churches across the country have requested copies of the video of the service that introduced what has become known as "The Austin Awakening." The move has been characterized by intense worship and a deeper hunger for God.[12]

Lord, Open the Heavens

I believe our only hope is a full-fledged, heaven-sent move of God that must begin somewhere with someone. It happened in 1859 in New York City with a forty-six-year-old businessman named Jeremiah Lamphier. All he did was call a noontime weekly prayer meeting where business people could meet for prayer. They began at the Old North Dutch Reformed Church on Fulton Street on September 23, 1857. The first day there were only six businessmen who showed up, and not all on time. But within six months there were hundreds of thousands of people praying in 150 prayer meetings across Manhattan and Brooklyn.[13]

Let us be clear here. We are not seeking Elijah; we are seeking Elijah's God. What we need in the church in America is "a permanent break from nominal living."[14] We are calling a hiatus on sin and negative thinking, realizing that the God of the Bible—the God of Elijah—the God of fire is moving across the world.

"Do we want to be sidelined during the next move of God on America?"[15] Or can we as pastors and leaders across America step into a God-given destiny and avail ourselves anew with the Baptism of Fire?

It is the Holy Spirit that will cause us to live above the ordinary plane of life—the same Holy Spirit that turned the apostle Stephen into a firebrand for God (Acts 6:8).

Smith Wigglesworth said, "Never live in a place other than where God has called you, and He has called you from on high to live with Him." He also said, "Pentecost is the last thing that God has to touch the earth with."[16] If we are living without the Baptism of Fire, we are living impoverished Christian lives.

For the majority of Christian history, the church has underestimated the power and influence of Pentecost. We have turned it into an observance on the liturgical calendar that we respectively recognize once every twelve months. We may beef up the Sunday morning litany and drape the place in red, but we do not really experience the dunamis (dynamic) power that was released fifty days after Passover.

My contention is, even though we tend to underestimate the effect of Pentecost, it really is difficult to overestimate it. In that one event God birthed the church and released a witness to the Christian Gospel that literally transformed the ancient world for 350 years. Kingdoms toppled and cultures yielded to the influence of the Holy Spirit working through a Spirit-baptized church.

I believe we are again at the point in history where kingdoms are toppling and cultures are yielding to the very potent influence of the Holy Spirit working in a Spirit-ignited church, a church born of Fire. After preaching all across America the last twenty years, I know the average church desperately needs the Fire. God is calling us in America to be that church. Can you hear His voice? Will you, too, climb that mountain and challenge the death and darkness that is strangling our culture and our nation?

We are farther down the history of this world than we know. The time is now to be the prophetic voice with signs following, and to rescue a nation that has gone whoring after other gods. I challenge and summon the church in America to witness the God who answers by Fire.

Chapter 2

Making Tracks in the Trenches

I suppose surviving thirty years in the ministry is an accomplishment in itself. But surviving in the same church for thirty years, while seeing a move of God . . . well, that is something else. It is practically unheard of for a United Methodist pastor to stay in the same church for thirty years. Most remain for five or six years, and then are moved to another location.

My journey in renewal has been colorful and high energy. I am blessed to pastor a Spirit-filled United Methodist Church that is power-packed and full of grace. In our atmosphere, people are constantly "bitten" with the ministry bug. At least one person per year takes steps toward full-time Christian service. It wasn't always that way.

However, I want to begin with a story from the year 1988. I was at the United Methodist Annual Conference in Lakeside, Ohio, doing what most people do at annual conference: renewing relationships and moving about through the crowd. There I was, at the back of Hoover Auditorium, when a woman began struggling with the drinking fountain. Apparently, she had turned the knob, but only a little bit of water squirted out, hardly enough to quench her thirst. She turned around to the person behind her and remarked, "This drinking fountain works about like our church . . . it doesn't!"

I thought how many laypersons and pastors have had the same feeling about their own churches? Considering the woman at the fountain was a delegate to the conference—no doubt an active member—I began to wonder what the average person in the pew must feel these days. What is the "take away" from our Sunday morning services? What impression do we want lingering in their minds and hearts? Each pastor has to consider these questions seriously.

Humble Beginnings

I began ministry at Trinity Church in Pickerington in June 1973. Fresh out of seminary and wet behind the ears, I really was in over my head. I can still remember standing behind the sacred desk in the pastor's office with that initial sense of awe and humility. Even today, thirty-two years later, I feel those same emotions. It is a great responsibility to preach the Word of God and to lead a congregation to a deeper relationship with the Almighty.

My wife, Linda, and I felt very inadequate in the beginning. I can remember kneeling with her in the parsonage study, praying, "Lord, teach us; use us in this place. We desperately need you." As we continued to pray, we felt His sweet presence and His anointing. Through prophetic word He gave us great hope for what was about to take place.

In 1973 Trinity Church was rural. Situated in northwestern Fairfield County, it was bordered by corn and soybean fields. It was a fabulous place to raise our three children. Like so many places in rural Ohio, it had its own ethos, and we were about to "learn the language." It was very different from our home surroundings in Dayton, Ohio. We were city kids about to be given a whole new education. "In the faith" some things are opposite from "in the world." In Christianity you get the degree first, and then you get the education.

My first year, the church's annual budget was $35,000 and we had about ninety people in attendance. Prior to my arrival, Trinity had shared a pastor with another Methodist church in town. It was a two-point charge. However, six months before I arrived, the congregation decided to become a "station church" and break away from the other church to become a single charge. In a sense, I was Trinity's first full-time pastor, and the church was ready to grow.

What Is Growth?

At first, the congregation's only vision for growth seemed to be this: If we can get people to come into this building who look like us, think like us, and talk like us, then they can be a part of us. Of course, that is not what God had in mind; but at least the people were willing to grow, and the door was open.

Lyle Shaller, a well-known church analyst, has said that each generation of the church has to take out a new franchise. The church is always in flux, always changing in its witness to an unredeemed world. We should never feel threatened by the constant movement all around us. Our God is on the move as well, and so our church began to move and change.

The early years were a combination of relationship building and preaching a clear word on Sundays. I witnessed folks receiving Jesus into their hearts right in their own living rooms. We would pray and kneel at their sofas, and I would lead them in a "prayer of acceptance." I took Isaiah 55 as my umbrella.

> As the rain and the snow come down from heaven, and do not return to it without watering the earth and making it bud and flourish, so that it yields seed for the sower and bread for the eater, so is my word that goes out from my mouth; it will not return to me empty, but will accomplish what I desire and achieve the purpose for which I sent it (Isaiah 55:10–11).

If I was going to be committed to building a church, then I had to leave my personal agenda at the doorstep and ask God to reveal His divine agenda to me.

I believe in a revelation lifestyle. We cannot find our marching orders in *Time* magazine, college courses, or even seminary. Our lifestyle must be contextual. My thought here is that Jesus is the Head of the church. We must find His will for each local church, and then work that field with all of our strength. Leadership must have a vision. This is the most important principle I have learned. God must bring a vision for the work.

Like my good friend Mike Slaughter, pastor of Ginghamsburg United Methodist Church, has said:

> Church renewal is more than an increase in numbers and budgets. Many gimmicks can be employed to persuade people to come and sit in a church pew. Church renewal consists of people in community with one another, dreaming God's vision, believing Christ's victory and living out the Spirit's work.[17]

I have discovered that a vision is not something we find, but something that finds us. When it does, we write it down (Habakkuk 2:2). Furthermore, everyone can seek God for a vision. Each person has a vision from God to discover. Your vision is waiting for you to find it. The initial vision that God gave me for the local church was the church at worship. I wanted to see a church with people more interested in the Lord than just filling an hour on Sunday. I saw people with uplifted hands, excited about being together, excited about blessing and praising God. I heard their sweet sound of worship flowing together, and I saw an awesome symmetry of order and spontaneity.

God gave me that vision for my church when there was absolutely no evidence that during the next five years it would ever take place. There were times I did want to leave and move on. Every pastor has to fight through these things—perhaps the salary raise was not enough, or people gossiped about you, or the hours of work were too long.

Yet God kept me there, glued to the vision. It was as if I wasn't carrying the vision, but the vision was carrying me. God said, "Scott, roll up your sleeves, trust my word and preach it. I have given you a vision and I am going to fulfill it. If you are not in this with everything you have, then you have nothing to be in it with." Do you know a vision has always been very important to God's people?

The Power of Vision

Before going into Jericho, Joshua had a vision of the angel of the Lord. In Joshua 5:13, he said, "Are you for us or for our enemies?"

The angel answered, "Neither, but as commander of the Lord I have now come." On the road to Jericho, Joshua received the battle plan and went on to conquer the city.

In Exodus 3, Moses saw a vision of the Lord. The reality of the burning bush—whatever it was—became a powerful manifestation of the presence and the will of God. That vision propelled Moses to become the person he thought he could never be.

In 2 Kings 6, at the siege of Samaria, Elisha also had a vision. He told his servant Gehazi, "Open the man's eyes that he can see that those that are with us are greater than those that are with him" (v. 17). Throughout history, the concept of vision has been vital. The Word says, "Where there is no vision, the people perish." (Proverbs 29:18, KJV)

In turn, God gave me a vision for the church, and I was determined to see it through. I continued to preach and teach the Word, and the church began to grow. People who looked, dressed, and thought a little differently than the rest of the congregation made their way to the little white country church. After time, they began to demonstrate their differences, and the fermentation process began. In the midst of it all, people were being born again and filled with the Holy Spirit, and the vision began to take shape. The church was growing.

After three years of conservative growth, we had a lay witness mission in the church. This was a weekend experience whereby a leadership team assembled from around the country to provide a spiritual shot in the arm. Boy, did it ever! It became a strategic and wonderful experience. By 1978 we made some changes in the music, purchasing a new hymnal called *Hymns for the Family of God*. A spirit of revival broke out in the church and everything accelerated—the giving, the attendance, and the mission. We began to plan for the future.

The original structure of our church was built in 1866. A basement was dug in 1946, and a modest side addition was added in 1964. By 1979 we were at multiple services and launched into a massive remodeling the next year, tripling our capacity. I can remember well the day we dedicated the building in 1981. The Bishop stated upon his approach to the church, "Here is another opportunity to preach in one of our little country churches." When he arrived, every seat was filled, all five hundred of them. Later the Bishop admitted, "It blew my mind when I saw your sanctuary. It was much bigger on the inside than it looked on the outside."

Again, I give all the credit to God and the preaching of His Word. I have been a kind of teaching evangelist over the years. Every time we instituted any changes in the church, I would teach on it so that the emphasis would be on the Word and not on me. A very wise evangelist, Dr. Lon Woodrum, wrote me a letter that said preachers are sword-slashers. When they get done with a sermon, there can be a lot of bleeding. But teachers are like surgeons; they heal as they cut. There is pain in renewal, but it leads somewhere positive.

The Seven Principles of Renewal

Early on, I read a book titled *Brethren, Hang Loose* by Robert C. Girard. In it he lifted up seven principles of New Testament church life.[18] I have used these principles throughout my ministry because I see them to be universal and normative in the life of a local church. There are some things that just "work" in the life of a church, and these work. They are as follows:

Principle #1—The Headship of Christ and the Unity of the Body (1 Corinthians 10:17 and 12:12, Ephesians 1:22–23, Colossians 1:18, and others)

Jesus Christ is the Head of the church, and we are the body. This is not intended to be a metaphor. He really is the Head of the church. It is the responsibility of the Head to communicate to the body. The single most important thing that we do in our local churches is to comprehend what the Head is saying to us. It is very possible to do that if we wait on the Lord.

The second most important thing, once we find out what the Head is saying to the body, is to do it. There are simply too many options available and no church can do all of them. What is it that God is calling us to do? Find it, my friend, and you will find life.

Principle #2—Recognize the Priesthood of the Believer (Exodus 19:1–6, Hebrews 4:14, 1 Peter 2:5, Revelation 1:6 and 5:9–10)

Every local church needs to operate out of the understanding that we are all priests of the Lord. We are not all clergy, but we are all ministers of Christ. For years, on the first page of our church bulletin, the leadership was identified as the entire congregation.

One of the biggest mistakes pastors make is to insulate themselves from others and their gifts. We should not be threatened by laypeople. We need to surround ourselves with the best possible people who have gifts, anointings, and administrative abilities that we ourselves don't have. Then the job of the pastor is to turn these people loose to minister under the anointing of the Holy Spirit.

When Trinity Church discovered this one principle, it revolutionized ministry in our body. Applying this principle frees the pastor to be about his or her calling and lets others "take the ball." Ministry will explode under this principle. It becomes very exciting.

Principle #3—Concentrate on the Maturing of Christians (Ephesians 4:1–6, Colossians 1:28)

There is a desperate need for people to grow in the Lord. Our destination is Ephesians 4:13 ". . . until we all reach unity in the faith and in the knowledge of the Son of God and become mature, attaining to the whole measure of the fullness of Christ." We pastors are helping people grow toward a goal. Believers are also to be the "sent ones" to a world waiting to see the "real deal." The unbelievers know when they encounter the real thing.

Principle #4—Depend on the Holy Spirit Instead of the Flesh (Galatians 5:16–26)

The work of the church is a supernatural work. If what we are called to do is not beyond our reach, except for the intervention of God the Lord, then our goal is not high enough. Church can deteriorate into meetings, schedules, and events, all of which lose their continuity and purpose without the higher calling. We are called to touch and wash the feet of the world for Jesus' sake. Let us honor our unseen Partner in all that we do.

Principle #5—Release Church Life from the Confines of the Building (Hebrews 9:11–14)

Such things as home group ministries, prison ministries, and a host of other "off-site" meetings can reinforce the idea that church is beyond the walls of the sanctuary. For instance, on the first Wednesday of the month we take a hot meal to the homeless in downtown Columbus, and minister to their spiritual needs as well. We must go to the world; the day is over when the world comes to us.

Principle #6—Recognize Your Place in the Total Body of Christ (1 Corinthians 12:12–32)

The reason God may allow the denominational expressions to continue is that each one brings a truth to the table that the rest of the body of Christ still needs to hear. Each denomination has a place, and if we seek the mind of Christ, that place will become known.

Principle #7—Build Church Unity on the Basis of Love (1 John 4:7–12, 1 Corinthians 13:1–7)

Love is the framework that holds the entire structure of the church together. Without love we may have a structure, but we will not have the church. It is the greatest of the gifts and is to be sought with endurance. Love never fails.

These seven principles played an important role in the renewal of Trinity Church. We continued to progress, and after five years things really started to roll. Those were five years of praying, sweating, and working night and day. In another situation, another church, I don't know how long it would have taken. I learned to roll up my sleeves, put my hand to the plow, and not look back. Today one can experience our worship service and no matter whether he is in the faith or not, he will be touched by God. And that is good.

I have also learned there is no quick fix; no one-two-three set of spiritual maneuvers that will transform a body of believers into an army of God. Yes, we can learn from the Rick Warrens and the Joel Osteens—but their experience will not be ours. A person must go directly to God and receive the battle plan for his or her situation. I think it is a combination of biblical principles and being led directly by the Holy Spirit which will take our churches into the next dimension.

I sense that is what the author of Proverbs means in 4:7: "Wisdom is supreme; therefore get wisdom. Though it cost all you have, get understanding." This can only come from God. Please do not misunderstand this next statement. I am all for education, but in a way, it breaks my heart to see pastors scurrying around the country to this conference and that conference, trying to extract the next thing that will make their church grow. The best we can do in any temporal conference is share horizontally. What the church needs in the 21st century is a vertical touch from God Almighty. This, I am convinced, is essential.

Struggles Are Inevitable

Over the years I have struggled in certain areas that may at least bring some encouragement to leaders in the trenches. The first one is patience. Sometimes we have to be *willing* to be patient before we can *be* patient. In the vast majority of cases this process takes time. God is not in a hurry. He would rather you get it right than get it soon.

At times God moves at a snail's pace, and other times He moves so fast we're in a whirlwind and not sure what is happening. But God has a pace, and we must get in step with His pace. Rather than one-two-three and out pops a growing church, it is pray, stay, and day-by-day. Church growth is full of ideas on how to tinker with the structures. We Americans want to reduce a vital church down to the "right method." Then we can package it, market it, and away we go. However, my experience suggests that God does not change structures; He changes people, and this change takes time.

"We look not to the things that are seen, but to the things that are unseen" (2 Corinthians 4:18 RSV). Perhaps this is a reality that will help us get in the mindset for patience—the temporal versus the eternal. Structures are temporal; people are eternal. Remember, everything we do not see is more real than everything we see. The best part is that our unseen Partner is always there.

Another struggle I have found in leading a church in renewal is that there are many strange people drawn to the light. There are times when I plead to the Lord, "God, why do I get all the weirdos? Haven't I been good? I pay my taxes, love my wife, and am not into pornography. What is the deal?" However, I have learned there always will be people like that in and out of the body of Christ. We try to help them as best we can.

We also better know the difference between sheep, goats, and wolves. Sheep follow; goats but-but-but; wolves destroy. Years ago an evangelist told me, "You feed the sheep, milk the goats, and drive out the wolves." The wolves in sheep's clothing can destroy a church if we do not have our discernment tuned into the Lord. I have had to be very direct with some people over the years for the sake of the larger body of Christ. The pastor needs to be firm and exercise leadership in these situations. God will back your play.

A third area of struggle is resisting the temptation to compromise principle. There are places to compromise in dealing with human beings, of course, but not on principle. For example, early in my ministry I remember watching members of our church raise a major portion of the annual budget through fundraising activities such as dinners, bake sales, and rummage sales.

Our women's group rented a storefront in the poor section of the inner city. Who knows from where they collected mounds of rummage and then sold it to these poor people, thinking they were doing them a favor. As I stood there watching them collect the money, I got a sick feeling in my stomach. I said, "God, there has to be a better way." I wondered if the last pastor of the church was asleep at the switch. We should be giving this stuff away, not selling it!

I began teaching and preaching on tithes, offerings, and alms—the three modes of giving practiced both in the Old and New Testaments. The challenge went forward and the people responded to change. We never had financial problems after that. A meager budget soared to $400,000 a year and kept climbing every succeeding year. God's people need a challenge. Today we only allow a very limited amount of fundraisers that are over and above the budget of the church—usually done by youth groups for missions. The total budget is raised by tithe and offering alone.

Nuggets of Insight

Finally, I want to share a few nuggets that will help every pastor and leader stay on target over the long haul. Remember, the Christian life is not a sprint, it's a marathon. These things must be in place all the time if we are to achieve long-term success in ministry.

Our first obligation in ministry is to minister to the Lord. I am not talking about a quick prayer during cereal in the morning. I am talking about quality time with God every day. I am convinced this is the Achilles heel in the ministry. We allow ourselves to get too caught up in the mechanics of ministry while we neglect the Lord of the ministry. Unless what we do is God-breathed, it will not produce lasting results. In Acts 6, the apostles commissioned seven disciples to "serve tables," so that they could spend their time in "prayer and the ministry of the Word."

Jesus said, "Without me you can do nothing," and "I am the vine, you are the branches" (John 15:5). If we do not abide in the Lord and come apart, we will simply fall apart. The dropout rate in the ministry today is horrendous. Pastors and leaders are dropping like flies. They are tired, worn out, and spiritually exhausted because they have neglected this principle. And friends, there is no way around it. You either take the time, or time will take you. Jesus modeled this behavior (see Matthew 14:23, Mark 1:35, Luke 6:12). He is our Leader; let us follow Him!

We must realize that we never get done in ministry. There will always be something else to do before you go to bed at night. However, the Gospel of John states that Jesus fulfilled the task that God the Father had given Him (John 17:4). How can this be, when there are still prostitutes walking the streets and people with leprosy dying? Because He had done what the Father had asked Him to do, His work for that day was done. He had "the spirit of knowledge and the fear of the LORD" on Him (Isaiah 11:2).

Bill Gothard of the Institute in Basic Youth Conflicts has defined "the fear of the Lord" as "the continuous awareness that one is in the presence of a just, holy, and righteous God, and that every thought, word, action, and deed is open before Him and being judged by Him."

The second nugget I want to share is the priority to minister to our spouses. That which God has bequeathed to us in marriage is precious, and we need to nurture it regularly. Our family must take priority over the needs of the congregation. If we do not have a good marriage, the people will know and the ministry will suffer.

How pastors and leaders treat their spouses in the midst of the flock will teach more about marriage than any series of sermons. Ephesians 5:21 describes marriage as a relationship of mutual submission. Both husband and wife may not be called to be a minister, but both must share the call.

The Holy Spirit bestows four kinds of gifts on the spouses of pastors:

1. Gifts of the **heart**—kindness, understanding, forgiveness, and commitment.
2. Gifts of the **mind**—memories.
3. Gifts of the **Spirit**—prayer, vision, and direction.
4. Gifts of **communication**—encouragement, inspiration, and creativity.[19]

Normally, your spouse will be with you long after the kids leave the home and the church hangs your picture in the vestibule with your successors. A deficit in this area will lead to bankruptcy down the road. Let's get it right. Many a ministry winds up on the ash heap because of this neglected loyalty. We must do better in marriage.

The final nugget may not come as any surprise to you: expect resistance when making major moves forward in the life of the church. There is a real enemy, and he is committed to opposing the ministry of Jesus in the world. We must possess a "spirit of never give up," and possess the zeal of the Lord as we take ground. Matthew 11:12 says, "From the days of John the Baptist until now, the kingdom of heaven has been forcefully advancing, and forceful men lay hold of it."

In 1984 we purchased thirty acres of land across the road from the original church for future expansion. We paid $90,000 cash on land contract. This was money raised over and above our budget. We immediately began the process for rezoning the land for church use. A civic association opposed this request to the township trustees, and it took us four years to finally get the zoning. Following our victory, a citizen neighbor sued us, the zoning commission, and the township trustees over the decision.

One year later we prevailed in the courts, but my point is, battling for our rights will carry the day. The "free ride" for the religious community is over in America. The infrastructure no longer sees the church as its friend. We are going to have to take ground, and we had better know which fight to fight.

Finally, after three years of fund raising, we broke ground for our new family life center. Seating over one thousand people and with 31,000 square feet, it was worth the battle. We now have a ministry facility that is used day and night by the entire community. We have plenty of room for expansion, and the ministry landscape is secured for years to come. Hopefully, we will be worthy of all the Lord has entrusted to us. Our God is lifted up; let the enemies be scattered!

Chapter 3

The Cosmic Catalyst

There exist many metaphors and analogies when describing the work of the Holy Spirit from a New Testament perspective. The many "hats" that the Holy Spirit wears in bringing the church into conformity to the purpose of God is truly amazing. A while back, I began to see the Holy Spirit as a kind of catalysis in His work among the church.

The word "catalysis" refers to "the causing or speeding up of a chemical reaction by the addition of some substance which itself undergoes no permanent chemical change thereby."[20] The Holy Spirit undergoes no change, yet itself effects change when intermingled with our faith walk.

With the Holy Spirit resident in our lives, we do not need special circumstances or conditions to fulfill the will of God. The only thing we really need is obedience. Samuel said, "Does the LORD delight in burnt offerings and sacrifices as much as in obeying the voice of the LORD?" (1 Samuel 15:22). If we will hear, and then obey, we will truly see God move in our churches. Since one cannot see the Holy Spirit, we must observe His effects as we track Him through history. Note these brief examples:

- Genesis 1:2—"Now the earth was formless and empty, darkness was over the surface of the deep, and the Spirit of God was hovering over the waters." In the beginning, earth was void and the Holy Spirit began to move across that void and bring definition to this creation called earth. The Hebrew word here for Spirit is *Ruach*, which means "wind." Similarly, when the Holy Spirit comes into the void of our lives, He brings purpose and definition. There is a significant amount of void in modern day society.

Bob George, a seasoned Christian counselor and radio host, has made this observation: "What makes a man different from an animal? What could it mean that man was created in God's image? I found the answer in the spiritual aspect of man. The human spirit is the part of man that enables him to relate to and know God, and is the source of his inner drives for love, acceptance, meaning, and purpose in life. Man's spirit was created to be united with God's Spirit and was the means through which he originally enjoyed perfect fellowship with God."[21] It takes the Spirit of God to bridge the gap.

- Exodus 31—Bezalel and Oholiab were craftsmen filled with the Holy Spirit to render beautiful furnishings for the tabernacle of God in Moses' day. These were gold, silver, bronze, stone cutting, woodworking, etc. They did not only quality work, they did unbelievable work.
- Numbers 11:16–17—God took the Spirit that He put on Moses and put it on the seventy Elders. As a result, they began to prophesy and minister in a similar anointing—a kind of pre-Pentecost, if you will. Suddenly Moses was multiplied seventy times! In the upper room the Holy Spirit fell and multiplied Himself 120 times! The Holy Spirit always increases everything He touches.
- Ezekiel 37:9–10—The Wind of the Spirit blew into an army of dry bones and they became animated. "Then he said to me, 'Prophesy to the breath; prophesy, son of man, and say to it, This is what the Sovereign LORD says: Come from the four winds, O breath, and breathe into these slain, that they may live.' So I prophesied as he commanded me, and breath entered them; they came to life and stood up on their feet—a vast army."
- Luke 4—It was the Holy Spirit that anointed Jesus to step into the prophetic declaration of ministry known as Mes-

siah. When He came out of the Jordan River after being baptized by John the Baptist, Jesus began functioning immediately as the Messiah of Israel.

- John 14:12—Jesus declared to His disciples that they would do greater things than He had done because He was going to the Father. Additionally, He was going to send the "Spirit of Truth"—the catalyst—into their midst. This would amount to a worldwide witness to His truth all at the same time. How could it be?

All these and many more are examples of points in time mingling with the Cosmic Catalyst. The next example is perhaps the greatest display of the coming of the Holy Spirit to date. The implications of this encounter have carried the church for 2,000 years. It is called Pentecost.

Pentecost: Partnering With God

Pentecost was an Old Testament high feast celebration (Exodus 23:16, Leviticus 23:15–22, Numbers 28:26–31). It took place fifty days after the Passover. It was fixed on the calendar like our Christmas or Easter.

It was a time of harvest, in gathering the firstfruits from the fields. It was called the "Feast of Weeks" or the "Feast of Harvests." It was when Jews assembled in Jerusalem to present their firstfruits to God. In it they blessed and thanked God for a new time of bounty.

Isn't it interesting that Pentecost blew in a new season of "spiritual harvest" with the birth of the church. Three thousand were added to the church in the first day. Hear again the record from the Book of Acts:

When the day of Pentecost came, they were all together in one place. Suddenly a sound like the blowing of a violent wind came from heaven and filled the whole house where they were sitting. They saw what seemed to be tongues of fire that separated and came to rest on each of them. All of them were filled with the Holy Spirit and began to speak in other tongues as the Spirit enabled them. (Acts 2:1–4)

What I want us to see is this: Prior to Jesus' birth, we had a prophetic understanding of the ministry of Messiah, but there were still many gaps. All the words in the world were not like the actual Person standing there in front of the believers. When He was born, and later when He grew up and assumed His ministry, the people could actually see what Messiah was like. He did heal the sick, raise the dead, and cast out demons. He displayed His miracle-working power, His wisdom in teaching, and His tender compassion for the downtrodden.

Here we have a similar scenario with the Holy Spirit—prophetic revelation prior to His coming; expectancy, yet some ambiguity. However, when the Holy Spirit actually fell, He was on display for all to see, in and through the church. The work of Jesus was accelerated 120 times. The whole church began to heal the sick, raise the dead, and cast out demons, and from that moment mushroomed into the most significant force for change in the ancient world.

A Big Event

The coming of the Holy Spirit is as big of an event as the coming of Jesus. We don't really think of it that way. The whole culture shuts down for Christmas and Easter, but Pentecost . . . huh . . . what is that? Most of us have to check the calendar each year just to confirm the date. But I ask you: What would we do without the Holy Spirit? Where in the world would we be? What if Jesus would have said prior to His ascension, "Okay, I have done my part. Now you figure it out from here"? Instead, He said:

"I will not leave you as orphans; I will come to you." (John 14:18)

"And I will ask the Father, and he will give you another Counselor to be with you forever." (John 14:16)

"I have told you now before it happens, so that when it does happen you will believe." (John 14:29)

Jesus really wanted us to have the Holy Spirit. He wanted us to understand the significance of the third Person of the Godhead. It was the Holy Spirit that would navigate the church through the murky waters of history until He comes again. I heard Billy Graham say that the leaders of the world's other religions and philosophies were unable to promise that they would never leave their followers. Ours did!

It was the Holy Spirit who would fill His followers with power from on high. They would receive Him in the Baptism in the Holy Spirit and walk in His anointing. You see, before Pentecost the emphasis was on the word "ask" (Luke 11:9). After Pentecost the emphasis was on the word "receive" (Acts 2:38). We are no longer waiting on the Holy Spirit; He is waiting on us.

One of the great church historians of our day seems to confirm these observations. C. Peter Wagner, who has been studying growing churches for the better part of forty years, has made this observation: "I noticed that the churches worldwide that seemed to grow the most rapidly were, for the most part, those that outwardly featured the immediate present day supernatural ministry of the Holy Spirit."[22]

Waiting in Anticipation

The ancient prophets held out the hope that every devout Jew longed to see. Ezekiel's words were truly prophetic. "I will give you a new heart and put a new spirit in you; I will remove from you your heart of stone and give you a heart of flesh" (36:26).

The result of such a divine transplant would be the birth of a new people who would go to the ends of the earth to establish His kingdom. "But you will receive power when the Holy Spirit comes on you; and you will be my witnesses in Jerusalem, and in all Judea and Samaria, and to the ends of the earth" (Acts 1:8).

We are talking about a very versatile person here. You have

heard the phrase, "that person wears many hats." Well, so does the Holy Spirit. Here are some characteristics of the Holy Spirit:

He speaks—Rev. 2:7, Acts 13:2	He can be grieved—Eph. 4:30
He intercedes—Rom. 8:26	He is eternal—Heb. 9:14
He testifies—John 15:26	He is all powerful—Luke 1:35
He leads—Acts 8:29, Rom. 8:14	He is everywhere present— Ps. 139:7ff
He commands—Acts 16:6–7	He is all knowing—1 Cor. 2:10–11
He guides—John 16:13	He is called God—Acts 5:3–4
He appoints—Acts 20:28	He can be lied to—Acts 5:3–4
He is the Creator—Gen. 1:2, Col. 1:16ff	

Not to mention He is the Comforter, Counselor, Guide, Teacher, and Friend. This third Person of the Trinity can flat get the job done. When we become the yielded vessel, God can distribute the gifts as He wills, and the work of the church will prevail in history.

Peter Hocken, Executive Secretary of the Society for Pentecostal Studies, reminds us, "The spiritual gifts make heaven more real." And "the reappearance of the full range of these gifts makes more evident the *heavenly* character of the kingdom of God."[23]

Keeping this in mind, the principal way to think about the Holy Spirit is not that He is our resource to help us get done what we want done. Rather, we are His resource to help Him get done what He wants done. If we can keep that thought straight, we will have a wonderful journey in the Holy Spirit.

Harvest Evangelism

The nations of the world are waiting to be harvested by the gospel of Jesus Christ. This is a clear mandate in Scripture, and the missionary infrastructure to make it happen is intact. Unless we keep Pentecost and the experience of the Baptism in the Holy Spirit connected to harvest evangelism, not just to an individual experience, we will miss the greater purpose for which it was given. Remember, the original mandate was to "be my witnesses (martyrs) in Jerusalem, and in all Judea and Samaria, and to the ends of the earth" (Acts 1:8).

Note the progression in the gospel accounts:

- "Therefore, go and make disciples of all nations, baptizing them in the name of the Father and of the Son and of the Holy Spirit" (Matthew 28:19).
- "Go into all the world and preach the good news to all creation" (Mark 16:15).
- ". . . And repentance and forgiveness of sins will be preached in his name to all nations, beginning at Jerusalem" (Luke 24:47).
- "Peace be with you! As the Father has sent me, I am sending you" (John 20:21).

Four out of the above five quotes emphasize the intentional global push of the evangelistic task. When you add Matthew 24:14—"And this gospel of the kingdom will be preached in the whole world as a testimony to all nations, and then the end will come"—it would be difficult here to miss the central emphasis: *carrying this Word to the ends of the earth.*

The vision statement of the church I pastor reflects this mandate. Our vision is to:

Become a community of true disciples under the Lordship of Christ, born of the Holy Spirit, driven by passion for the Word and the worship of God, filled with the love of the Father, and witnessing to the saving power of Jesus in our city and to the nations, until He comes again.

Light at the End of the Tunnel

There is a time line involved in the propagation of this gospel of the kingdom. Salvation history is linear, and there is light at the end of the Great Commission tunnel. Do you realize that our generation is the first since this mandate was issued twenty centuries ago to reasonably see its conclusion?

Most of us in "pew land" have heard the term, the 10/40 window. It is the "area of the world between latitudes 10 degrees and 40 degrees north of the equator, covering North Africa, Middle East, and Asia. The window has in view most of the world's areas of greatest physical and spiritual need, most of the world's least reached peoples and most of the governments that oppose Christianity."[24]

It used to be that if a person was born in the 10/40 window he would not have the possibility of hearing the gospel in his lifetime. Today a baby born in the 10/40 window will have a reasonable chance of hearing the gospel in his lifetime. God has linked the power of the Holy Spirit to world evangelism, and we must do the same. This is the maturing that has come to the charismatic renewal.

Barrier-Breaking Experience

There is no question that the Baptism in the Holy Spirit has brought an awareness of His presence and power that is dynamic and sustainable. This remains what the church needs at this hour of history—a sustainable presence of the Lord which renews the individual and everyone in their corridor of influence. The Holy Spirit will leave none untouched.

In order to begin the Great Commission, the first believers had to cross barriers. In Acts 2, they broke the barrier between Hebraic Jews and Hellenistic Jews. In Acts 8, they broke the barrier between Jews and Samaritans through Philip's ministry in Samaria. In Acts 10, Peter broke the barrier between Jews and Gentiles in the house of Cornelius.

What is interesting to me is that in two of the three episodes, speaking in tongues was a predominant factor. This could become a paradigm of how the kingdom of God would be spread around the world until Jesus returns. Tongues was a characteristic resident in the experience, and I believe it is still today.

The Great Commission came on the heels of Pentecost and began establishing the kingdom of God among the nations. (See Acts 1:3; 28:31.) Would it not be wonderful if every church in America got bit by the "missionary bug" and targeted an unreached area of the world? I believe the 21st century church will close the window on the Great Commission and we all can be a part of it. I urge each person reading this book to go to prayer and specifically ask the Lord for the nations of the world, and for your part in the harvest.

And While You're at It . . .

And while you're at it, ask the Lord for a new, fresh Spirit-baptized touch of His power in your life. In Acts 1, the church took its greatest step forward while standing still. One could ask, how can that be? The watchword was *wait.* Don't move; just wait for the promise of the Father. If they had gone forth without being energized by the Spirit Baptism, they would have fallen flat on their faces in failure. Of this I am convinced.

Part of the frustration with modern-day ministry, including the pervasive dropout rate, is that we are trying to do ministry in our own strength and not in the strength of the Holy Spirit. As Francis MacNutt says:

> We talk a good game. We believe true doctrine. But most of
> us have never learned to seek and receive the baptism with
> the Holy Spirit and to exercise the gifts of the Spirit.[25]

We must be Spirit-saturated and anointed to do this work. The power (*dunamis*) is still available to every Christian believer. Forget the labels; forget the denominational affiliations; and forget the prejudice of theological posturing. God wants you, and He is a jealous God. He wants all of us.

Think of it this way. The Baptism in the Holy Spirit is not about how much of the *Spirit* you have. It is all about how much of *you* the Spirit has. When we are fully, totally yielded, God turns on the power. After all, each Gospel records the necessity of the Baptism in the Holy Spirit (see Matthew 3:11, Mark 1:8, Luke 3:16, John 1:33).

I was told in seminary, if three out of the four Gospels recorded the same story, it probably really happened (not my hermeneutic). Well, guess what? All four Gospels include this imperative for the church, including Acts 11:15–16. That's a homerun in my book.

I can truly say that my experience of being filled with the Holy Spirit was as dramatic as my salvation experience. It was there that I received the "fuel" for the journey. After thirty-two years of continuous ministry, I can honestly say I look forward to Sunday mornings at Trinity Family Life Center. I can't wait to get there to experience the corporate worship in the power of the Holy Spirit; the spontaneous flow of God during the services, which sometimes significantly alters the direction of the service; and the presentation of the Word of God, which has creative power in itself to heal the sick, mend the sinner, and restore the broken hearted. Every Sunday morning there is at least one person in our service who is desperate for a word from God. We need to be on the point anticipating— ready to throw a lifeline to another human being and realize the harvest that is at hand.

Why don't you cry out right now and ask God for a fresh anointing in your life? Allow the wind (*ruach*) of the Spirit to blow in and blow out the cobwebs of stress and care. Go ahead; move forward by standing still, and wait until you receive "the promise of the Father." It will change your life.

Chapter 4

A Safety Net for Renewal

Aldersgate Renewal Ministries

My ministry over the last thirty-two years has been marked by a deliberate participation in parachurch groups, as well as the local church. One of these parachurch ministries which has been a tremendous influence in my life is Aldersgate Renewal Ministries (ARM). These next pages are meant to give the reader a history of ARM and the wonderful influence it has had all across the church.

I believe groups like ARM can provide a "safety net" for those interested in the renewal of the local church. They provide opportunities for teaching, fellowship, and strategy development, as well as a larger covering of prayer for the ongoing effort of renewal, while slugging it out in the local church environment. Being a part of a larger renewal effort helps to provide context for ministry and hope for the future.

To understand ARM, we must begin in the Book of Acts 1:4, 8.

> . . . Wait for the gift my Father promised, which you have heard me speak about. For John baptized with water; but . . . you will be baptized with the Holy Spirit . . . you will receive power when the Holy Spirit comes on you; and you will be my witnesses . . . to the ends of the earth.

Aldersgate Renewal Ministries (ARM) was conceived at the Conference on Charismatic Renewal in the Christian Churches (CCRCC) in 1977 as The United Methodist Renewal Services Fellowship, Inc.

(UMRSF), ARM held its first national conference on the Holy Spirit—Aldersgate '79—in Louisville, Kentucky in August of 1979. Although the legal name is still UMRSF, the working name of the ministry was changed to Aldersgate Renewal Ministries (ARM) in 1995.

Much of the early history is drawn from an unpublished paper entitled, *A Brief History of the UMRSF*, prepared in 1994 by William P. Wilson, MD and Ross Whetstone. However, before ARM was fanned into flame, the wind was already blowing through: (1) The Pentecostal/Charismatic Movement; (2) The Lay Witness Movement; (3) Development of *The Guidelines: The United Methodist Church and the Charismatic Movement;* and (4) CCRCC, Kansas City, July 1977.

The Pentecostal/Charismatic Movement

In the preface of his book, *The Century of the Holy Spirit: 100 Years of Pentecostal and Charismatic Renewal,* Dr. Vinson Synan says, "Beginning with a handful of students in Topeka, Kansas, on New Year's Day, 1901, Christians around the world have experienced a renewal of the gifts of the Holy Spirit that dwarfs anything seen since the days of the early church. This movement, which now constitutes the second largest family of Christians in the world (after the Roman Catholic Church), is found in practically every nation and ethnic group in the world. By the end of the 20th century over five hundred million people were involved in this revival which continues its massive growth into the new millennium."[26]

Synan goes on to describe the basic distinctions between the Pentecostals and charismatics. "The Pentecostals," he says, "were the people who pioneered and popularized the idea of a baptism in the Holy Spirit with the necessary sign of speaking in tongues. In the early days of the century they were expelled from the mainline denominations and forced to found their own churches. Some scholars now call them 'classical Pentecostals.'"

The term *charismatic* was first used around 1963 to denote those 'neo-Pentecostals' in the mainline Protestant and Catholic churches who also spoke in tongues but who did not see tongues as the necessary evidence of the Pentecostal experience."[27]

Although there were no clearly recognizable national charismatic leaders, and no organization or "charismatic renewal fellowship" among United Methodists (as there was among the Roman Catholics, Episcopalians, Presbyterians, Lutherans, Mennonites, etc.) until 1977, another phenomenon was occurring—primarily in Methodism—called the Lay Witness Mission.

The Lay Witness Mission

The Lay Witness Mission (LWM) began in 1960 under the leadership of a United Methodist clergyman named Ben Johnson, operating the Institute of Lay Renewal under the aegis of Emory University. As an alternative to traditional revival services in a local church, a team of lay witnesses would share their faith over the course of a weekend in a variety of settings in the local church. The closest thing to preaching would be when the team coordinator shared his or her testimony on Sunday morning, with an invitation for the attendees to commit their lives to Jesus Christ as Lord and Savior.[28]

The LWM has been an extremely effective tool of evangelism for thousands of United Methodist churches. There is no way to measure how many tens of thousands of people experienced a new birth as a result of having a LWM in their church.

I scheduled a Lay Witness Mission at Trinity in the fall of 1975, just a few years after I had been appointed as pastor. The rubbings of change had already begun, and some folks were feeling a bit threatened by this new young upstart pastor with his talk about the Holy Spirit. However, following the Lay Witness Ministry, a beautiful atmosphere of commitment and love pervaded the church and provided the seedbed for the real renewal to take hold a few years later. The Lay Witness Mission definitely ignited fires at Trinity.

The Lay Witness Mission, not a single leader, was the primary vehicle that God used to introduce United Methodists to the Lordship of Jesus Christ and to the working of His Holy Spirit. At its peak in 1973–74, Danny Morris, then Director of Emerging Ministries of the *Upper Room*, reported that the General Board of Discipleship (GBOD) had scheduled 2,400 Lay Witness Missions per year from the Nashville office. Many others were being scheduled from other places like Atlanta, Georgia, and Wilmore, Kentucky. At that time, it is reported that there were in excess of 100,000 team members on the rolls in Nashville who were available to the 1,200 coordinators for use in missions.

Many of these folks, and some congregations, were experiencing charismatic renewal. What would the denomination do with these spiritually renewed Christians who continued to worship in United Methodist churches?

Sadly, the United Methodist Church did not know how to deal with the dramatic change that took place in the lives of the laity. Because of their zeal and enthusiasm, they were often seen as a divisive force. Often efforts were made to stamp out the movement. The result was that these renewed persons went underground or outside the church to experience and exercise the gifts of the Spirit. Their thirst for more of God and their desire to learn more about the work of the Holy Spirit resulted in participation in para-church groups such as Full Gospel Business Men's Fellowship (FGBMFI), Camps Farthest Out, and meetings held by Pentecostal churches and charismatic organizations.

During the early 1970s, at the height of the Lay Witness Movement, Dr. Ross Whetstone served as the Assistant General Secretary of the Section on Evangelism for the General Board of Discipleship of the United Methodist Church, and was responsible for managing the lay witness movement. He recognized the need to do something to utilize the power possessed by these renewed people. He wanted to mainstream the energy into the church as a whole.

Unfortunately, many Methodist charismatics held a Pentecostal interpretation of the Scriptures relating to the gifts of the Spirit because of their contacts with FGBMFI and Pentecostal churches. That is, they believed the doctrine of "initial evidence" to the Baptism with the Holy Spirit was the gift of tongues. This was not seen as compatible with Wesleyan theology.

Many charismatics left Methodist churches for Pentecostal and independent charismatic churches. To stem this exodus, an official statement on the role of the charismatic renewal was desirable. Such a statement could indicate to the church at large that they were not an aberration and should be nurtured.[29]

The 1976 Guidelines

In 1972, the Western Pennsylvania Annual Conference made a request of the General Conference of the United Methodist Church (UMC) for a position statement on the charismatic movement and the UMC. Rev. Dick Burns, then a pastor in Johnstown and later appointed as a General Evangelist from Western Pennsylvania, was a prime mover in the request. The General Conference referred the request to the General Board of Discipleship Section on Evangelism.

As the head of evangelism, Ross Whetstone chaired the committee assigned to formulate and write the position paper called: *Guidelines: The United Methodist Church and the Charismatic Movement.* This paper was adopted by the 1976 General Conference as the denomination's official position relating to the charismatic renewal and the operation of spiritual gifts. Ross came out of a Salvation Army background and was personally acquainted with the person and work of the Holy Spirit. Dr. Robert Tuttle was instrumental in writing significant sections of the paper.

Simultaneously, the church needed enlightenment concerning this most recent movement of the Spirit. To accomplish this, the General Board of Discipleship (GBOD) organized and executed a series of conferences across the country whose express purpose was to teach and demonstrate the person and work of the Holy Spirit in the Wesleyan tradition.[30]

Kansas City, July 1977

The Conference on Charismatic Renewal in the Christian Churches (CCRCC) brought together an estimated fifty thousand persons from at least thirteen major Christian denominations, and up to forty smaller groups and networks. The event was planned and organized by the Catholic Renewal Services. It was an amazing gathering with Roman Catholics, mainline Protestants, Pentecostals, Independents, and Messianic Jews sharing in leadership and worshipping together in one place. Contemporary historians claim it was the largest ecumenical gathering in the history of the church. The leadership and attendees were classified as coming from four main streams: Catholic, Pentecostal, mainline Protestant, and Non-Denominational. They came together to celebrate the Lordship of Jesus Christ and their common experience of the outpouring of the Holy Spirit.

Since the UMC did not have an organized charismatic group, the GBOD deputized Ross Whetstone to organize and lead the United Methodist portion of this historic event. By then, Ross had left his position at the GBOD to teach as a professor of Evangelism at Scarritt College in Nashville, Tennessee.

Ross invited four other United Methodists to join him in providing leadership for the United Methodist section of the Conference: Dr. Robert G. Tuttle, Jr., who was a professor at Oral Roberts University; Dr. Robert Stamps, who was serving as chaplain at Oral Roberts University; Rev. Tommy Tyson (deceased 2003), who was a General Evangelist from North Carolina; and Dr. William P. Wilson, who was a professor of psychiatry at the Duke Medical School. These five men of God would later become the "founding fathers" of the United Methodist Renewal Services Fellowship, Inc. (Aldersgate Renewal Ministries).

It was estimated that about eight hundred Methodists attended the conference. During a question-and-answer period at the United Methodist sessions, several concerns were discussed. The issue of whether the United Methodists should form a national fellowship group within the denomination was discussed at length. It was strongly encouraged by the attendees, who felt alone, isolated, and disenfranchised from the general church. Even though all five of the leaders were opposed to such an idea, those gathered in Kansas City pressed the issue until the leadership agreed to take the matter to prayer for six weeks and report back by mail.[31]

Gary Moore, present Executive Director of ARM, and his wife Sally were part of the United Methodist contingent that attended the CCRCC in Kansas City in 1977. At that time, as lay leadership of the First United Methodist Church of Bedford, Texas, Gary was employed by Texas Utilities Company in Fort Worth. One of the things God spoke to those present in Kansas City was, "You will experience soon a release into full-time service to build up the body of Christ." Upon returning home, the word was confirmed by several other people, including Gary. The following June, he left Texas Utilities (after thirteen years) to join the staff at the church where his family had been members since 1972.

Organizing the UMRSF

Upon his return to Nashville, Whetstone consulted with Bishop Earl Hunt—then resident Bishop of the Nashville area—about the formation of a renewal group. Bishop Hunt answered without hesitation, "You must do it!" The next week, Whetstone met with Bishop James S. Thomas, who also encouraged him to start the renewal group. With the reassurance gained from the encouragement of two bishops, the five leaders from the Kansas City conference met later in 1977 in Chapel Hill, North Carolina, to launch the UMRSF.

As they sought the leadership and wisdom of the Holy Spirit in their deliberations, there were several things that seemed clear to them: (1) They would go forward only if they could affiliate with the General Board of Discipleship (GBOD). They were to work within the structure of the church to bring about renewal in the power of the Holy Spirit. (2) They were to remain non-political and non-adversarial in their efforts for renewal. They desired to be characterized as "lighting candles" rather than "cursing darkness."

In early 1978 there was a second meeting in Chapel Hill, with invitations being extended to potential candidates for board members. A board was appointed, a constitution and by-laws were adopted, and officers were elected. A Board of Directors and an Advisory Council, with representation from each of the five regions/jurisdictions, were elected over the next two years. Dr. Wilson was elected as the organization's first President, and Whetstone was hired as part-time Executive Director.

From the beginning, the group sought to be related to the GBOD as an affiliate organization and was granted that status in a covenant relationship in November of 1978. ARM is the only mainline renewal group that has an official, "connected" relationship to its denominational structure.

Pioneers

Dr. William P. (Bill) Wilson was the only layman among the original five founders. He had served as a coordinator for over one hundred Lay Witness Missions. In the mid-1970s, he was a professor of psychiatry at Duke Medical School. Later, he would enter a full-time ministry of counseling, teaching, and healing as the head of the Institute of Christian Growth.

Dr. Wilson was elected as the first President of the ARM Board and served from 1978 until 1983. Under his leadership, the renewal organization was formed, secured its affiliation with the GBOD, held its first national conference, opened its first office, and hired its first Executive Director. In 1979, the first Aldersgate Conference was held in Louisville, Kentucky. The intent was to sponsor an annual, national conference on the Holy Spirit. The name, *Aldersgate*, was used to tie the event to John Wesley's "heart-warming" and life-changing experience with the Holy Spirit, the Spirit of Jesus Christ (see Chapter 5).

The Aldersgate conference, as well as the organization, is rooted in the experience, tradition, heritage, and theology of the Wesleys'. Over the years, the Aldersgate conference has become a reunion for Spirit-filled United Methodists from all across the country. It is a constant reminder to the denomination of its need for the presence and power of God's Holy Spirit in the life of the church. Aldersgate is one of the largest voluntary gatherings of United Methodists in North America. Aldersgate is a "connecting place" for Spirit-filled United Methodists who feel called to stay, pray, and work for renewal of the UMC by the power of the Holy Spirit.

The event, bathed in prayer, is characterized by its joyful praise and worship, powerful preaching and ministry, and anointed teaching—particularly related to the person and work of the Holy Spirit, the Spirit of Jesus Christ, and His role in building up the church, the body of Christ. In 1980, ARM opened an office in the United Methodist Center in Nashville, and Whetstone became its first full-time Executive Director. (For those interested, an expanded edition to this history can be obtained from ARM, 121 East Avenue, Goodlettsville, Tennessee 37072; www.AldersgateRenewal.org).

Your Latter Will Be Greater

Harry and Ann Peat and I served as the co-chairs for the planning committee for Aldersgate 1980 in Columbus, Ohio. This is how I officially began my time with ARM. I was also part of the leadership for the first international mission team sent out from ARM as they helped inaugurate the Aldersgate Conference in the Philippines in 1996. That conference continues to be a blessing to hundreds of pastors and laity each year. I have also represented ARM, both nationally and internationally, in ecumenical charismatic meetings.

My term as President of Aldersgate Renewal Ministries began as a very trying time for the ministry overall. This same period of time also proved to be one of the most challenging in my own personal life. My father had just experienced a major stroke, and I had to intervene, with many trips back and forth to Dayton, Ohio, where my parents lived.

At the same time, I had a trusted staff person fall into sin, which affected the entire church. In addition, I was assuming leadership of a city-wide pastoral network in Columbus, called the Capitol City Association of Ministers and Churches, with over 200 churches and para-church ministries attached to it. I was also doing a good bit of public speaking across the nation, as well as being the senior pastor of my own church. It all was a stretch, but God was faithful. I have a magnificent staff at church, which really makes the difference in my life at these times.

In the spring and summer of 1998, I had the awesome responsibility of leading the most crucial board meetings in ARM's history. It looked and felt like the death of a vision. The financial support for ARM seemed to dry up the last quarter of 1997 and the first quarter of 1998. There didn't seem to be any explainable reason; it just happened. The Executive Committee met in April, unsure that we could stay in business until the Aldersgate '98 conference scheduled in July. The question posed at the first meeting: Is God finished with this ministry?

- If He is, then we need wisdom to know how to shut it down without bringing dishonor to the kingdom of God.
- If He isn't, then we need courage and boldness to press forward, and we need wisdom to know what to change in order to live into His corporate destiny for ARM.

We prayed together; then we dismissed to pray over those questions through the night. We were to return the next morning to hear what God was speaking to each person. There wasn't much sleep that night.

The next morning, there was a consensus that God was not yet finished with ARM. It was unanimous that He had not completed the work we were called into existence to accomplish. Everyone heard that we needed to regroup and press on. We needed to seek God for a fresh vision. So, we eliminated any unnecessary spending. We laid off one staff member and cut all remaining salaries by 15 percent. We sent out a plea to our constituency; we let them know our financial situation; and we asked for their prayers and support as we continued to seek God for the future. The following is an amazing testimony, written by Gary Moore, to the great turnaround of ARM:

Two weeks later, my wife and I went to our oldest granddaughter's first piano recital at the Goodlettsville Nazarene Church. Even though we had lived in the community for seven years, we had never seen this church and had to get directions. It turned out to be only two blocks from our current offices, tucked away in an older residential area and invisible from normal traffic routes. As we walked toward the sanctuary that morning, I noticed a "For Sale" sign in the front yard, and the Holy Spirit came upon me as I walked into the building.

Throughout the recital, I was having visions of people in worship, in ministry, and receiving ministry in that building. During the reception, I excused myself, walked back through the building and around the building, asking the Lord, "What is going on? What does this mean? What are you trying to say to me?" It was very clear. "This is your building. I am going to give it into your hands. My plans for you are a future and a hope."

It was the birth of a vision. But who was I going to share it with? I shared with my wife, Sally, and with my daughters and their husbands, but felt no release to share with staff or Board members. I began to experience a season of visionary dreams that lasted through the end of the year about how God planned to use the building to expand ARM's ministry.

Two weeks before Aldersgate, a man in another city shared with Sally and me that he had this humongous business venture in the works, and that when it materialized, God was telling him to give ARM $1 million. He was going to come to Aldersgate and slip the check under my door. This gift never did materialize, but it was used by God to fan the flickering flame of faith in my heart to consider that He was doing something beyond my own thoughts and imagination.

I couldn't help but wonder if the building and the promise of a million dollars were connected. So, I called the real estate agent and went to look at the building (pray my way through it). The week before we left for Aldersgate '98, I shared with the staff what was going on with me, and took them over to look at the building. I didn't want them to be totally shocked if I came home from Aldersgate with a million dollars and a building to buy. None of this made sense to any of us, since we were still having trouble making payroll and paying the bills.

I also shared with another couple who lived out of state and who were always present in my recurring dreams about this property. I just shared what was going on and asked them if they had any discernment about what it all meant. They didn't have a clue, but agreed to join me in prayer.

During the Executive Committee meeting, as we were trying to decide how we were going to pay off the note on our little building (the doctor wanted the balance of his money and was calling the note, with an outstanding balance of about $110,000), one of the Board members blurted out, "I think we just need to sell that little building and buy something big enough to do ministry in."

Everyone was speechless, especially me. I was asking the Lord if this was an open door to share what had been going on between Him and me. He seemed to say "Yes," so I did. The consensus was to wait for further confirmation before sharing it with the full Board and Council.

Between the Executive Committee meeting and the full Board and Council meeting, Sally and I had lunch with the out-of-state couple I had confided in. They wondered if I had shared my vision with the Executive Committee. I told them how it had come up and what had happened. They looked at one another, and then began to reveal how excited they were about the possibilities of expanding the ministry of ARM. They were so excited that God was leading them to give 50 percent of the cost of the property as a matching gift challenge. The asking price for the property and buildings was $750,000. I was stunned!

We called a sidebar Executive Committee meeting, and decided this was enough confirmation for us to move forward. After sharing with the Board, Scott called everyone to prayer. When we reconvened, the response of the people was to begin making pledges. The place was electric with excitement for the future. By the time the meeting was over, more than $80,000 had been pledged. We never did vote on whether or not to buy the property.

At the 1998 Board meeting in Dallas, the ministry also refined its purpose statement to read: "The purpose of ARM is to encourage United Methodists and their churches, by the grace of God and the love of Jesus Christ, to be filled, gifted, empowered, and led by the Holy Spirit in ministry to the world."

When we returned home from Aldersgate, the realtor called me to say that since I had looked at the building before leaving town, the Board at the Nazarene Church had received a prophecy that said "they were standing in the middle of a miracle, and that ARM was supposed to have the buildings." He was authorized, on behalf of the church, to reduce the asking price from $750,000 to $665,000. In addition, they would give us $175,000 for our existing building as a down payment, and they would self-finance the balance. They asked if they could stay in the building and pay us rent until their new one was completed. Only God could give that kind of favor or negotiate that kind of deal!

We closed on the building in November 1998 and had the buildings paid for by the time we moved into them in September of 1999. In the interim, we drew up plans for a $500,000 renovation and furnishing the buildings to transform them into the Aldersgate Renewal Center and office headquarters. Even though we moved into the buildings debt free, the debt for the renovations hung over us until December of 2004.

In November 1998, before we took possession of the building, ARM hosted a group of pastors who claimed to be interested in the renewal of the church. It turned out that they were extremely wounded, discouraged, and angry. Many of them were more interested in finding a way to leave the denomination and to do as much damage as pos-

sible on the way out. I had invited a young man named
Jonathan Dow to assist me (as music and worship leader)
in leading this group in a 24-hour concert of prayer. Scott
Kelso and Margie Burger were also present to pray and assist in leadership. God moved in an amazing way—healing,
restoring, and encouraging many of the broken pastors in
attendance.

What we witnessed that week of prayer planted seeds of vision
for ARM's future Pastor and Spouse Retreats, as well as deflected a
major schism throughout the entire denomination. Many of those
pastors were angry and confused with issues around the leadership
of the United Methodist Church. By the grace of God, the Holy
Spirit softened their hearts and convinced them to remain in the
church and work for renewal.

Life in the Spirit

One of the core ministries of ARM has been a "Life in the Spirit"
weekend seminar for the local church. Team members are assembled from around the country and dispatched to a local church,
with activities beginning on a Friday evening. Participants are exposed to teaching, fellowship, and instruction, as well as opportunities to "go deeper" in their experience with the Holy Spirit. One
such weekend was written up in *Ministries Today* some time ago.

The leadership of the Harmony-Zelienople United Methodist
Church (HZUMC) had scheduled a seminar for the weekend of
February 28 through March 1, 1992. Even though many of the people were a bit apprehensive with having all these "strangers" come
into their church, they forged ahead under the leadership of their
pastor, John Seth.

Pastor Seth had actually been preparing the congregation
for years, through balanced biblical preaching that included
the person and work of the Holy Spirit. As the seminar approached, a core group of about fifteen people made a

commitment to fast for up to two days (a new experience for many), and to spend those mealtimes in prayer for the weekend.[32]

The church secretary reported that many of the people were struggling with some mixed emotions of anticipation and fear. However, on Saturday evening, "as the Holy Spirit filled the sanctuary and I felt His presence, all of a sudden it didn't matter anymore what anyone else was doing or thinking. All that mattered was that I would be obedient to what the Holy Spirit wanted of me. As we went forward to pray and be prayed for, there were tears of release and joy. There was also laughter—a lot of joyous laughter."[33]

The chairperson of evangelism, Ken Wilson, summed up the weekend this way: "The Holy Spirit ministered to each of us uniquely, as only the Holy Spirit can. He brought salvation, emotional healing, and physical healing. He met various individual needs. He provided victory over fear, pride and other sin. He dramatically demonstrated that He is a Spirit of love and peace, gentleness and power. We shared a Pentecost experience, and that same Holy Spirit still seeks to fill and empower each of us—those who were present, and those who were not—even today."[34]

This, then, represents the "safety net" for renewal, which titles this chapter. There is a place folks can go for encouragement and solid teaching around the experience of the Holy Spirit, which can be used to take churches "deeper" in the Lord than they have previously been. The experience at HZUMC is being multiplied hundreds of times across our nation. Churches and pastors are coming alive to the ministry of the Holy Spirit in a present day, main-line denomination, with no sign of waning.

Summary

Since my time as President of the Board of Directors of ARM, the Lord has expanded the vision of ARM, and additional significant ministries have been birthed. The following represents a brief summary:

- Total remodeling of the Aldersgate Renewal Center in April of 2000, with the entire debt eliminated by 2004.
- ARM Endowment Fund created through a matching gift challenge by a "million dollar donor." The Endowment Fund will allow ARM to continue developing ministries and resources that carry life-transforming power to pastors and local churches.
- A local church renewal event entitled *Lord, Teach Us To Pray* was developed by Margie Burger, the National Prayer Coordinator for ARM.
- A Pastor and Spouse Retreat weekend, inaugurated November 6–9, 2001. This event ministers to pastors and spouses for a weekend of meals, gifts, teaching, and date night, with no expense other than a modest registration. Many leave healed, restored, and renewed through the power of the Holy Spirit. As of this writing, 165 pastors and their spouses have participated in eight events.
- The development of an *International and Cross-Cultural* mission program, with outreach to the Philippines, Paraguay, Poland, and Africa. I was privileged to be a part of the first team to go to the Philippines in 1996 to launch "Aldersgate in the Philippines."

In June, 2004 the Lay Witness Mission Movement was transferred from the Board of Discipleship of the United Methodist Church to the auspices of ARM, and events are now being scheduled from the ARM headquarters. With a fourth local church renewal event titled "Worship in Spirit and Truth," ARM can now provide for four sequenced renewal events at nine-month intervals, and provide over a three-year period a process for renewal in every congregation in America. These events are not limited to United Methodists alone.

I want us all to see the value of a larger renewal network like ARM, in providing a wonderful "safety net" for the renewal of the local church. Many pastors feel isolated and alone in ministry. This no longer has to be the case. One of my purposes for including this chapter in the book is to let as many people as possible know what a tremendous life-breathing, passion-seething organization ARM has become. The flame in my local church has been fanned by ARM, which incidentally remains one of the best-kept secrets in the United Methodist Church. It is time to blow its horn!

Chapter 5

Calvary—
The Heart of It All

Bruce Shelley, in his well-written history of the Christian Church, begins the book with these words: "Christianity is the only major religion to have as its central event the humiliation of its God. Crucifixion was a barbarous death, reserved for agitators, pirates, and slaves." And Cicero (106–143), a Roman statesman, orator and writer said, "Let the very name of the cross be far, not only from the body of a Roman citizen, but even from his thoughts, his eyes, his ears."[35]

As I write, it has been one year since the showing of the worldwide-acclaimed movie, *The Passion of the Christ*, directed by Mel Gibson. This movie has been one of the biggest box office draws in movie history and the eighth largest-grossing movie ever. It has also evoked a firestorm of controversy and criticism, being labeled by the media elite and others as anti-Semitic. One thing is for sure, its graphic visual portrayal of the passion, suffering, and death of Jesus Christ will live on for decades. No other portrayal in history has come close to it.

When Pope John Paul II was asked about its presentation, he said early on, "It is as it was." It is hard to imagine anyone seeing this film and not being impacted by the force of the trauma and suffering of Jesus. We know that this "Christ event" has become the focal point of Christianity. I believe the 21st century church is ripe for a fresh encounter with the all-encompassing sacrifice of Jesus of Nazareth as they incorporate it in their daily faith walk. How is it that this one event, which occurred in the backroads of the ancient world, has such an unrelenting influence over this planet?

A Divine Stroke of Genius

One reason the cross of Christ is so controversial is because it is so comprehensive. Think about it. Theologically, it settles the matter forever of man's guilt on the one side and God's provision to forgive on the other. In one six-hour period, from 9:00 in the morning until 3:00 in the afternoon, every religion generated by man had become obsolete. No other offering, no other good work, no other religious posturing of any kind could bring merit or add to the cross of Christ. "For no one can lay any foundation other than the one already laid, which is Jesus Christ" (1 Corinthians 3:11).

In God's sight it was a resolute and definitive act of obedience that opened the life gate from God to man. Man is left to accept what God has done at Calvary or to remain unaccepted forever. Now that will cause controversy in anyone's book.

The Stigma of the Cross

Another amazing aspect of the entire passion of Christ is that Christianity survived the very real stigma attached to this method of death. The cross is a surprising symbol, considering the horror with which crucifixion was regarded. It was the cruelest method of execution ever devised, delaying death until maximum torture had been inflicted.

No wonder Paul's message of the cross was foolishness, madness to those who were perishing (1 Corinthians 1:18). How could any sane person worship as God a dead man who had been condemned as a criminal? This was seen as repugnant! The combination of death, crime, and shame put Jesus well beyond the realm of respect in the minds and hearts of His contemporaries.

In addition, the Old Testament cursed anyone who hung on a tree. "If a man guilty of a capital offense is put to death and his body is hung on a tree, you must not leave his body on the tree overnight. Be sure to bury him that same day, because anyone who is hung on a tree is under God's curse" (Deuteronomy 21:22–23).

The apostle Paul said in Galatians that Jesus became a curse for us. Peter reminds us that "He himself bore our sins in his body on the tree" (1 Peter 2:24). We must understand that the gravity of our sin must have been extremely horrible for God to allow a solution of this magnitude.

J. I. Packer has commented in his epic book, *Knowing God*, "All that has gone wrong in human life between man and man is ultimately due to sin, and our present state of being in the wrong with ourselves and our fellows cannot be cured as long as we remain in the wrong with God."[36]

The Remedy

Somehow the stigma becomes the remedy to man's predicament. R.C. Sproul, professor of systematic theology at Reformed Theological Seminary, brings us in for a close-up view. This death gate, this embarrassment, this cross of Christ "is a tragedy and a victory in the same moment. It is a scandal and an honor, a defeat and a triumph, a shame and esteem."

The predicament lies in the law. "Cursed be he who does not confirm the words of this law by doing them" (Deuteronomy 27:26 RSV). How can it be, when no human being has ever continued to do everything the law requires? Only Jesus has displayed this kind of comprehensive obedience. No one is justified by the law because no one has kept it.

The Old Testament prophet Habakkuk did make a provision for "the righteous to live by faith." Theoretically, those who obey will live, but none will live because none have obeyed. The curse or judgment of God, which the law pronounces on lawbreakers, rests on us. This is the predicament of mankind. We have all sinned and fallen short of the glory of God.

Christ has redeemed us by becoming a curse for us and taking away our sin when He died in our place on the cross. As John R. Stott has said, "When God justifies sinners, He is not declaring bad people to be good, or saying that they are not sinners after all. He is pronouncing them legally righteous—free from any liability to the broken law—because He Himself, in His Son, has borne the penalty of their law-breaking."[37]

This is what theologians call substitutionary atonement. He voluntarily accepted the liability of our condition. The Apostle Paul says, "God made him who had no sin to be sin for us, so that in him we might become the righteousness of God" (2 Corinthians 5:21).

Again, Packer weighs in here because "Jesus Christ has shielded us from the nightmare prospect of retributive justice by becoming our representative substitute, in obedience to His Father's will, and receiving the wages of our sin in our place."[38] The cross of Christ has saved us.

The Gravity of the Cross

The Apostle Paul was a consummate scholar, theologian, and "extremely zealous for the traditions of my fathers" (Galatians 1:14). However, once encountering the Lord Jesus Christ and being changed by His power, he could never escape the gravitational pull of the cross and resurrection on his life. He could rarely think about anything else. He would always find a way to bring it up in a conversation. I am not so sure that is not God's plan for all of us.

In that one event of the cross and resurrection, the destiny of earth and heaven has been fixed, and man and history have been judged. The cross was the line of demarcation between a God who has fully exposed Himself as love incarnate and an adversary who has fully incremented himself as evil uncompromised. Everything else said or done in history stands in the shadow of that one conclusive stroke of divine favor—the cross and resurrection of Christ.

In the cross, the greatest injustice of history has become the greatest blessing one could ever know. Have you ever been cheated, maligned, and humiliated? Join Jesus. Have you ever been misunderstood, ridiculed, and ignored? Join Jesus. Have you ever been abused sexually, physically, or emotionally? Join Jesus.

The record states that Jesus was innocent of wrongdoing and undeserving of this manner of death. Pontius Pilate declared three times, "I find no basis for a charge against him" (John 18:38, 19:4,

6b). This is the one place Jesus is unique from all who have ever lived. Scripture attests to this over and over:

- Hebrews 7:26—"Such a high priest meets our need—one who is holy, blameless, pure, set apart from sinners, exalted above the heavens."
- 2 Corinthians 5:21—"God made him who had no sin to be sin for us, so that in him we might become the righteousness of God."
- 1 Peter 2:22—"He committed no sin, and no deceit was found in his mouth."

So, if there ever was an answer to man's dilemma, it has to be the cross; and the great thing is, the cross is for all. Leon Morris writes, "Because it is God who is working out His purpose in the events associated with Calvary, and because there is but one God, the salvation there wrought out is effective for all mankind."[39]

The Major Issues of Our Day

There are several major issues that the cross addresses. I call them constant reoccurring challenges in an individual's life. They are things we need that only God can give. If we try to live without these things, we are living in a deficit condition. What are they?

- **Peace** (John 14:27)—So many people would love to have this gift in their lives. It is supernatural in its manifestation. We must remember peace is not the absence of problems; peace is the presence of God. The things that are beyond our control are not beyond God's control. He can impart peace to us because He really is there. His name in the last verse of Ezekiel is Jehovah Shama—the Lord is there! We have peace because He left it for us. "Peace I leave with you." We also become "peacemakers" because the Prince of Peace lives in us.

- **Self-Worth** (Isaiah 43:1, 41:8)—Self-worth is a significant problem in the lives of many people. I have met hundreds of people who are down on themselves. They have failed in some realm of their life. They persecute themselves and cannot forgive themselves. They never measure up to what someone else thinks they should be. Sometimes they look for self-affirmation in the wrong places and with the wrong people. Even the Apostle Paul was tempted with this problem, until the cross blocked out its power (Galatians 1:13–16, 1 Timothy 1:12, 1 Corinthians 15:9–10).

  The cross forever dispels the error that we are not loved. We are indeed loved, and of much worth to God. Isaiah, speaking for the Lord God says, "I have called you by name, you are mine." Think of it . . . we belong because we have been chosen. It is one thing to join; it is quite another to be chosen. We are chosen in the Lord. This, of course, was made possible when Jesus came into our world uninvited and took our sin on the cross. Now we can know what it is like to exercise our option—for heaven. We no longer have to act out. We are the beloved of the Lord. Take it to the bank!

- **Victory Over Sin** (Romans 7:15ff, Galatians 2:20)—Listen friends, no one has to be homosexual, commit adultery, divorce, cheat, steal, or have ten thousand other dysfunctions. We need to hold out the hope of a transformed life. If we really are going to be the church, we have to give folks an option (Philippians 2:15–16).

  It was 267 years ago that John Wesley went most unwillingly to a meeting on Aldersgate Street in London and experienced victory over sin: "In the evening I went very unwillingly to a society in Aldersgate Street, where one was reading Luther's preface to the Epistle to the Romans. About a quarter before nine, while he was describing the change which God works in the heart through faith in Christ, I felt my heart strangely warmed. I felt I did trust in

Christ, Christ alone for salvation; And an assurance was given me, that he had taken away my sins, even mine, and saved me from the law of sin and death."[40]

What is so interesting here is that Peter Bohler, leader of the Moravian movement, kept encouraging Wesley. The Moravians were the only group in history to have a 100-year prayer meeting. It was the Moravians who had peace on the deck of the ship, while Wesley was beside himself during a horrific storm at sea.

Wesley kept asking Bohler—should I pack it in? I don't think I have the goods. Do you know what Bohler told Wesley? "Preach faith till you have it; and then, because you have it, you will preach it."[41]

Read what Francois Fenelon (1651–1715), a Catholic mystic in the School of Quietism, says about victory over sin: "Without the presence of God, change is enveloped in fear, for it is difficult when we see God point His finger. The challenge becomes seeing ourselves as we really are. Yet, until we have something worth dying for, we have nothing worth living for. We must be willing to drink from a cracked or chipped cup, for that is the essence of life.

"You asked for a remedy that your problems might be cured. You do not need to be cured. You need to be slain. Quit looking for a remedy and let death come. This is the only way to deal with the self. Be careful of that bitter bravery that decided to accept no comfort to your ego. Do not seek any comfort from self-love, and do not conceal the disease. Uncover everything in simplicity and holiness and then allow yourself to die."[42]

- **An Assignment** (Matthew 28:16–20)—What is commonly known as the Great Commission comes from the One who really has the authority. After all, Jesus shall cause every knee to bow; He holds the keys to death and hell; He was raised from the dead; and He alone has authority to judge the world. I know of no other human being with a résumé like this. He simply has no rival. Jesus has given every follower an assignment. We have dignity, purpose, direction, and passion. What else do we need?

- **An Eternal Future** (1 Corinthians 15:51, 15:32)—I have found this is a big deal to the post-modern generation. Many young people are extremely interested in life beyond this world as well as core-value questions. What they have experienced in this world has left them empty and dry. They are searching for something real. As Colleen Carroll reminds us in *The New Faithful*: "Amid the swirl of spiritual, religious, and moral choices that exist in American culture today, many young adults are opting for the tried-and-true worldview of Christian orthodoxy." Most of these young believers share some key characteristics, among which are:

  1. Their identities are centered on their religious beliefs, and their morality is derived from those beliefs.
  2. Their adherence to traditional morality and religious devotion often comes at considerable personal cost, and the sacrificial nature of these commitments is often precisely what makes them attractive.
  3. They yearn for mystery, and tend to trust their intuitive sense that what they have found is true, real, and worth living to the extreme.
  4. They are, for the most part, concerned with impacting and engaging the larger culture. Yet they are equally committed to living out their beliefs in the context of authentic communities that support them and hold them accountable.[43]

The present-day movement of God is sweeping people into an experience of these realities, and it is making a difference in the church. And to think, it all flows from the cross. The Trinity paid a great price to have a relationship with us. A way has been made for every individual, and that way cannot be unmade. The specter of everlasting life becomes more real with every passing year.

The Symbol of the Cross

It is no wonder that Christianity chose the cross for its symbol. Almost every religion has some visual symbol to remind the devotee of its belief or history.[44] For example:

- Lotus flower—Although used by ancient Chinese, Egyptian, and Indian cultures, today it is particularly associated with Buddhism. It denotes the wheel-shaped cycle of birth and death and the emergence of order out of chaos.
- Star of David—Modern Judaism's symbol of God's covenant with David and His throne being established forever, with the promise of a Messiah to descend from His lineage (2 Samuel 7:16).
- Crescent—Islam's phase of the moon, indicating a process of evolving toward final truth.
- Hammer and sickle—The Marxist symbol adapted in 1917 represents industry and agriculture, crossed to signify the union of worker and peasants, factory and field.
- Swastika—An ancient symbol of 6,000 years ago denotes the movement of the sun across the sky and the cycle of the four seasons. It was Hitler's symbol of the Aryan race, with their racial bigotry.
- The Cross—The Christian symbol since the 2nd century. Christians drew, painted and engraved the cross as a symbol of their faith. In AD 200, Tertullian, a North African lawyer/theologian and an early church father, said of the cross: "At every forward step and movement, at every going in and out, when we put on our clothes and shoes, when we bathe, when we sit at table, when we light the lamps, on couch, on seat, in all the ordinary actions of daily life, we trace upon the forehead the sign."[45]

Dr. Lon Woodrum—one of my mentors in the faith who has long since gone to be with the Lord—expresses the glorious truth of the cross in poetic form:

He Whose Name Is Love

When they lashed him with their
Ignorant insults,
How easily could he, who commanded
Cosmic legions,
Have quieted their noisy tongues.
When they opened his back with
Their senseless whips, *
And jammed the brutal briars down
On his head,
How quickly he could have scattered them
Like dirty leaves caught in a whirlwind.
But he turned his lonely,
Bleeding face
Toward the drawn curtains of the sky,
And prayed for men who murdered him.
When the human wolf pack howled
And hate and anger shook the world,
Only he whose name was Love,
Could stand in stubborn dignity,
With the blasphemy of spit on his face,
And with frightening forgiveness
Still shining in his look.

(Unpublished; used by permission)

The Undying Need for Repentance

A medical doctor will tell you an abscess must be lanced; otherwise there will be no cure. After seeing Mel Gibson's *The Passion of the Christ*, I believe that for many people in America, the lancing has begun anew. I am not talking about some sterile grabbing around in your soul or some masochistic self-humiliation but rather a Spirit-generated evaluation of our need for a Savior from sin.

I believe the knowledge that we need a Savior is precisely what Western Christianity has lacked the power and authority to produce, both in the church and in the culture. Western Christianity has been tainted and corrupted by enlightenment thinking, with its emphasis on reason, science, and progressive values. The church has been robbed of its power, its authority, and its message.

So God comes along and says, "I am going to anoint a Mel Gibson to do my work"—a kind of George Whitfield or John Wesley of the 21st century. Instead of riding on a horse with a Bible in hand, he is riding on a silver screen in Technicolor. This medium has for too long been co-opted by the liberal media, not only for entertainment but also for social engineering. Look for more of these kinds of wholesome movies in the days ahead. By the way, don't think that movies don't affect people. I never swam in the ocean again after seeing the movie, *Jaws*. Movies can and do affect for good or for evil.

The theme of repentance in the life and ministry of Jesus cannot be ignored. The first time Jesus appears in the first Gospel, the initial instruction He gives is to repent. If you remember, this was also John the Baptist's theme in preparing the way for Jesus. It becomes Jesus' constant and universal appeal—not just to the Scribes, Pharisees, and power brokers of His day, but even to the poor and oppressed, repentance is the key to eternal life. On one occasion Jesus even advises repentance in response to a horrifying tragedy (Luke 13:1).

Repentance means to turn away from the wrong road, to amend wrong living and wrong thinking. It is a regret or a remorse—a turning away from sin and back to God. As used in the Bible, it is equivalent to conversion. In the Greek, *metanoia* means "a transformation of the mind." In other words, rethink your life. This is where the early church began its journey, and it is where the contemporary church needs to return.

Lon Woodrum, a Methodist evangelist of the last century said, "There are a thousand roads that lead away from God but only one road that leads back: repentance." A true move of repentance will create in our culture what a weak and anemic church has failed to produce in the last 150 years. That is how long it has been since the last Great Awakening in America.

Perhaps Mel Gibson's movie, in consort with a renewed church in America, can be successful in calling many to the only road that leads back to God. This one thing is for sure: the first step in our healing is not being comforted, but taking a hard look at what needs to be cleansed inside us. As Frederica Matthews-Green has said, "The starting point for the early church was the awareness of the abyss of sin inside each person, the murky depths of which only the top few inches are visible."

Flying Upside Down

The American church needs a spiritual reform similar to what happened in Israel in the 7th century BC under Josiah (2 Kings 22:8ff). According to the record, the law was discovered in the temple during some refurbishing of the building, and the king basically said, "How could we have existed so long without his word?" Finding these ancient copies of the law reminded the king of how far they had strayed from the precepts of God and how persistent God was to keep them in view. It was like a sign to the king. This one event spawned a whole host of reforms across the nation, including covenant renewal among the people.

The church in America is being called back to the cross and repentance for a renewal today. George Barna (Barna Research) has written extensively about the disconnect among Christians between "what we say we believe" and "what we do." The fact is that what we know in our hearts about "living a Christian life" does not affect the way we live or make decisions. This is very disconcerting to me, because I have seen our culture plunge into darkness on my watch in the ministry. I, for one, am not ready to throw up my hands and say, "Whatever!" There is a way back to God.

Dallas Willard, in his book, *The Divine Conspiracy*, refers to this disconnect in discipleship as flying upside down. He says, "Recently a pilot was practicing high-speed maneuvers in a jet fighter. She turned the controls for what she thought was a steep ascent—and flew straight into the ground. She was unaware that she had been flying upside-down."[46]

This seems to be a parable on human existence in our time. We live in a day when evil is called good and good is called evil. We don't even know we are flying upside-down. This "atmosphere" also affects the church. Only the light that Christ brings can suddenly transform our world and cause us to fly right-side-up again. Through repentance and the cross, we can become the glorious church that Christ died to bring forth. His glorious church is the only one He will return to claim.

Chapter 6

Healing and Restoration

When the Apostle Paul ministered to the church at Corinth, he told them:

> I did not come proclaiming to you the testimony of God in lofty words or wisdom. For I decided to know nothing among you except Jesus Christ and him crucified. And I was with you in weakness and in much fear and trembling; and my speech and my message were not in plausible words of wisdom, but in demonstration of the Spirit and of power, that your faith might not rest in the wisdom of men but in the power of God. (1 Corinthians 2:1–5 RSV)

Every pastor and leader must know that this "demonstration of power" included healing, miracles, and a living testimony to a risen Savior. For the first 350 years of the church, the same "demonstration of power" resulted in establishing the body of Christ throughout the ancient world. As this happened, a considerable amount of the witness of the church was in the healing ministry.

Dr. Francis MacNutt, Director of Christian Healing Ministries in Jacksonville, Florida, in researching his new book, *The Nearly Perfect Crime—How the Church Almost Killed the Ministry of Healing*, said, "for the first three centuries following the Resurrection, Christians boasted that any ordinary Christian could heal the sick."[47]

In addition, this ministry of the people also included casting out evil spirits. In fact, Ramsay MacMullen, a professor of history at

Yale University, answers the question of how the early Christians were able to establish Christianity as the religion of the Roman Empire, when they had no political authority and were considered by many as suspect and illegitimate. He writes:

> In assessing the psychological climate, the feel of those times for the non-Christian population, account must be taken also of the topics in common currency. What items of experience were people talking about and passing on to their neighbors? The most likely items on the religious page concerned Christian holy men, miracles, exorcisms, healings, and wonderful things.[48]

Randy Clark comments in his School of Healing and Impartation workbook manual for training Christians in the healing ministry: "People became Christians because the God the Christians worshipped was more powerful than the false gods they had previously worshipped. This was evidenced in the power of God to heal, and especially in the deliverance ministry of the Christians. What differentiated the Christians was how rapidly they could bring deliverance to those needing it."[49]

The Fading Witness

The next logical question would be: What in the world happened to the healing witness in the church? Fifteen hundred years later, why are we not "doing the stuff," as John Wimber, founder of the Vineyard Church movement, used to say, for doing the works of Jesus? Why have we anointed doctors, psychologists, and psychiatrists as the high priesthood of healing in the 21st century?

Please do not misunderstand me. The medical profession has provided an invaluable service to the sick in the modern era. Perhaps 80 percent of the people in the church would be dead without their skills. Yet, they are restricted by the scientific worldview and remain ill-equipped to take healing to the next level.

There is a missing dimension, and that is the dimension of the spiritual/supernatural. How did we get in this place, and more importantly, how can we restore the healing ministry of Jesus back to the culture? Fortunately, there are signposts that point the way home.

The Demise of Healing Through the Centuries

The church began to retreat from the healing ministry around AD 350. Special groups, such as priests, still anointed people through the sacrament of "anointing the sick." But as time progressed, these rituals became restricted to those who were very sick and not expected to recover. It was seen as a sort of last anointing, and physical healing was no longer the purpose. It became a preparation for the journey beyond this world.[50]

With the advent of the Protestant Reformation in the 1500s, there was a return to biblical concepts lost in the previous one thousand years. However, they did not include physical healing through the supernatural. One of the reasons for that was John Calvin and many of the Reformers who held to a cessationist theology. They believed the miracles in the Bible were true, but after the apostles had died off, the age of miracles had ceased. We no longer needed miracles to establish the validity of the Word of God. We have the Bible in its entirety, and that was all that was needed. Many today still hold to this theological viewpoint, even in the face of much evidence that points to the contrary.

Moving ahead three hundred years, we now understand that the modern era has become the custodian of enlightenment thinking, not only denying the continuation of healing and miracles, but going even further to say that the stories in the New Testament, such as the feeding of the five thousand or Jesus walking on the water, never really happened at all.

Modern theologians such as Rudolf Bultman and the seminaries where they teach could no longer square the stories about Jesus within the reach of scientific credulity. To say that Jesus physically rose from the dead would be impossible to believe. Their worldview demands a more logical explanation. Consequently, they say what the writers of the New Testament were really trying to communicate was that Jesus, in a very real sense, lived on in the lives of those who followed Him. This becomes a way of symbolizing a deeper truth. Their understanding of faith expresses that truth through resurrection. The problem is this kind of rationale makes for a very depressing Easter Sunday, not to mention the Monday following.

The last one hundred years have produced a broad acceptance in theological circles of the historical critical method of biblical interpretation, demythologizing the miracles, denying the major doctrines of the faith, while undermining the very foundation of the Christian church. In professional circles, these are called form and redaction criticism—part of the higher criticism that became prominent beginning in the late 19th century.

It seems to me that higher criticism, which has been recognized for only one hundred years, could hardly be scholarship's last word on the subject. After all, there remains a broad range of variation within the "higher critical community," and one can put down roots at various points along a continuum. Furthermore, the last quarter of the 20th century witnessed numerous archaeological discoveries that tend to substantiate the validity of the biblical record. No doubt the future will bring even more.

> For example, the healing of a leper in Scripture stood for the healing of his spiritual leprosy—sin—rather than a supernatural healing of a physical disease. The multiplication of the loaves and fishes was not an extraordinary physical increase in bread and fishes; it probably recalled a spiritual event in which the multitude were so deeply inspired by Jesus that they gave away the excess food they had previously hidden away in their loose-flowing garments. In this way, everyone was fed—a miracle of love—which was an even greater miracle than a physical multiplication of loaves.[51]

This has left the church weak and inept to bear a supernatural witness to a waiting world. If a person has not been in a Pentecostal tradition, chances are he has had no exposure to the supernatural ministry of the Holy Spirit, either through teaching or experience. Consequently, not only the secular culture is uninformed, but the majority of Protestant churches in the West has denied the legacy of Jesus to the church.

Francis MacNutt, in interviewing over one hundred thousand people during his ministry, says that his best estimate is 97 percent could never remember their fathers praying for them when they were sick as a child, and 80 percent could never remember their mothers praying for them when they were sick. "Most ordinary Christians have never learned they can pray with the sick and actually expect healing to happen."[52]

Healing has been almost totally lost in the modern church—the culmination of centuries of neglect, theological dispute, doubt, and unbelief. The really sad thing is we have done this to ourselves.

The Tide Is Turning

I am most glad to report that in recent years there has been an ascendancy of the supernatural all over the world, with documentation accompanying it. The church is beginning to come alive again to her destiny. I can personally testify, after having served as president of a national renewal network for four years (1997–2001), the churches which are alive and vital across America in United Methodism are experiencing the supernatural. One of the legacies of the charismatic renewal (1960–1990) is that God broke into the denominational world with new power and glory. We did not have to change denominational affiliation to receive the greater fullness of the Spirit.

With the addition of the Third Wave in the body of Christ, healing and miracles are being extended in a greater measure. The Third Wave is believers who have been traditional evangelicals, but who have been kept at a distance for the better part of a century because they could not reconcile the Pentecostal distinction of a subsequent Baptism in the Holy Spirit initiated by speaking in tongues. Third Wavers believe that an adequate reserve of the Holy Spirit resides in them from their conversion and continual fillings.

"The gifts then are released by the believer simply 'going for it.'"[53] From all of this, we see God on the move in history, and a post-modern generation is being set up to receive the greatest outpouring of the Holy Spirit since Pentecost. Ice on Fire is a reality in America!

At every level we see the Holy Spirit breaking into our world and changing our paradigm. I am particularly encouraged with the experience of Dr. Charles Kraft, Professor of Anthropology and Intercultural Communication at Fuller Theological Seminary. Dr. Kraft recounts his conversion from mainline evangelical to embracing the supernatural with healing and miracles. He has come to understand that these outward manifestations are a regular part of advancing the kingdom of God.

Having served as a missionary under an evangelical mission society for the first thirty-eight years of his life, Dr. Kraft had always been skeptical of the groups that claim to work in "spiritual power." He says:

> Up until 1982 I would have considered myself possibly open to contemporary reports of miraculous events, but fairly anti-Pentecostal and skeptical of most charismatic testimonies of the miraculous.[54]

However, in January 1982, John Wimber was invited to teach a course at Fuller entitled "Signs, Wonders, and Church Growth." Professor Kraft decided to attend the class. To his amazement, he recounts: "We saw many people healed before our eyes because Wimber and his ministry team members asserted the authority of Jesus over whatever problems people came with. And in due time I began to claim the same authority and to experience similar results."[55]

From that time to the present, Professor Kraft maintains, "The only kind of Christianity in the New Testament is a Christianity with power—a Christianity quite different from what I experienced during those first thirty-eight years. What I am experiencing now is Christianity with power."[56]

The Biblical Basis for Healing

Just what does the Bible say about healing and the miraculous? Realizing there is not enough space here to do justice to the subject, let's go ahead and at least look at a few key passages. I would encourage everyone to do his own study with an open mind. The results may be amazing!

There are three key reasons why God delights in healing. The first is the self-revelation of God. He is a God who heals; it is His nature.[57] The Bible says in Exodus 15:26, "He said, 'If you listen carefully to the voice of the LORD your God and do what is right in his eyes, if you pay attention to his commands and keep all his decrees, I will not bring on you any of the diseases I brought on the Egyptians, for I am the LORD, who heals you.'"

Healing is part of the nature of God, just as are holiness, truth, justice, and mercy. Healing is what comes from Him to enlarge the witness of the people of God and to extend His kingdom on the earth.

Secondly, healing would point to a prophetic witness for recognizing the Messiah.[58] In other words, healing would authenticate and verify the life and ministry of Jesus. Perhaps most of us have a life verse, a particular passage of Scripture that just puts it all together for us. Jesus had a life verse, and He quoted it in the synagogue on the Sabbath when He publicly inaugurated His ministry. Here is what He said:

> The Spirit of the Lord is on me, because he has anointed me to preach good news to the poor. He has sent me to proclaim freedom for the prisoners and recovery of sight for the blind, to release the oppressed, to proclaim the year of the Lord's favor (Luke 4:18–19).

This is a quote from Isaiah 61. It is what His life is all about. Then He went about the rest of His life doing these things (see Matthew 8:16, 9:35, 10:8, 12:15, 13:58, 14:36, 15:30). This then becomes the template for the "people of Messiah."

Thirdly, we the followers of Jesus have been commissioned by our Lord to also heal the sick.[59] We are not even told to *pray* for the sick. We are told to *heal* the sick. Of course, the process involves praying, but the authority is there to see it through. We do not have to wonder; it is God's will to heal the sick. Nowhere in the New Testament do we see sickness and disease as an acceptable condition. Nowhere!

Frank Damazio, who pastors one of the largest churches in the Pacific Northwest, says, "Disease and sickness are not from God. We must renounce them and confess our trust in God and His Word."[60] Hear the testimony of Scripture:

> These twelve Jesus sent out with the following instructions . . . heal the sick, raise the dead, cleanse those who have leprosy, drive out demons. Freely you have received, freely give (Matthew 10:5, 8).
>
> When Jesus had called the Twelve together, he gave them power and authority to drive out all demons and to cure diseases, and he sent them out to preach the kingdom of God and to heal the sick . . . so they set out and went from village to village, preaching the gospel and healing people everywhere (Luke 9:1–2, 6).
>
> Therefore, go and make disciples of all nations, baptizing them in the name of the Father and of the Son and of the Holy Spirit, and teaching them to obey everything I have commanded you. And surely I am with you always, to the very end of the age (Matthew 28:19–20).

His Majesty Displayed in Dayton

Years ago I was preaching at a series of meetings in Dayton, Ohio, in Victory United Methodist Church. There was a good spirit in the church and the meetings were going well. One of the first nights I gave the altar call for healing, and a number of people came forward. One of them was a woman whom I would describe as "a little, old Sunday School teacher." I asked her how we could pray, and she said, "I have tumors in my breasts." Most people when hearing that would think, oh, this is the end of the line for this one.

However, when we prayed I felt the power of God go into her. It was a definite physical sensation. I probably have this sensation 30 percent of the time I pray for people. I can feel the energy of the Holy Spirit in prayer. This night it was particularly pronounced. After a time of prayer she returned to her seat. I had encouraged her, stating, "God touched you tonight." Her son and daughter-in-law accompanied her to the meeting. Her daughter-in-law had actually visited our church some time earlier when she was in central Ohio, but I did not know her.

This precious little woman returned to the meeting the next night and wanted to give a testimony. I said of course. She had been to her doctor that day, and he cancelled all procedures because there were absolutely no tumors in her body. She was totally healed! Needless to say, the place went wild! Shouting and clapping broke out, and people flooded to the altar for prayer. Salvations and healings continued through the end of those meetings.

All this seems to confirm what Carlos Annacondia, a powerful Argentinean evangelist says: "One of the main purposes for performing these miraculous signs is to save sinners and bring them back to Him. Jesus Christ did not divide his meetings into services of evangelization or healing services. In the ninth chapter of Luke, the Bible tells us that Jesus and His disciples went from village to village, preaching the gospel and healing people everywhere. They announced the message of salvation and also healed the sick."[61]

An interesting postscript to this event happened years later back in Dayton. About four years after my father died, my mother came to the point where she could no longer care for her home. We needed to put the house on the market. Lo and behold, the realtor she chose happened to be none other than Marge Miller, the daughter-in-law of the woman who was healed of tumors at Victory UMC. How good is God? I asked her about her mother-in-law. She said she lived several more years and finally died of old age, remaining totally healed of the tumors. It's not often that a pastor gets to follow up on these kinds of reports, and I found this very encouraging indeed.

The apostle Paul sees gifts of healing and miracles as gifts of the Spirit (1 Corinthians 12:9–10). This is interesting, because it perpetuates the actuality of this mode of working indefinitely. As long as there is a church, there will be gifts of the Spirit. After all, it is through the church that the gifts are exercised.

I believe the church is appointed and destined to live in the atmosphere of miracles. In Matthew 4, they brought all manner of sickness to Jesus. Why? He was not a doctor; He was a preacher. The kingdom He came to preach included the supernatural and spoke to all manner of human conditions. We should take heart and be encouraged. This bears the stamp of an authentic church taking ground from the enemy and extending the kingdom of God.

Father Dennis Bennett, by virtue of his own Spirit baptism, inaugurated the charismatic movement in the mainline denominations in 1960. He writes in his best-selling book on the Holy Spirit:

> So immediately after Pentecost we find the first believers continuing the ministry of Jesus in healing the sick, raising the dead and casting out evil spirits. Jesus' healing ministry has been going on now for nearly two thousand years, and will continue until He Himself returns to earth.[62]

The Church and Spiritual Warfare

There is no question that even a once-through reading of the New Testament portrays a powerful battle between light and darkness. Vinson Synan says, "The Scriptures indicate that, in the last days, there will be two revivals taking place at the same time—Satan's revival and God's revival—in one last great struggle to win the allegiance of the people of the world."[63]

John begins his Gospel with these words: "In him was life and that life was the light of men. The light shines in the darkness and the darkness has not overcome it" (John 1:4–5 RSV). Here John is positioning his theme that Jesus' ministry is a constant struggle between the kingdom of light and the kingdom of darkness.

Matthew's Gospel declares, "From the days of John the Baptist until now, the kingdom of heaven has been forcefully advancing, and forceful men lay hold of it" (Matthew 11:12). Again, light has a collision with darkness, and darkness will be exposed. When Paul is making his defense before Agrippa and witnessing to his conversion experience, he was convinced that God was launching him to the nations to be an ambassador for Christ.

The Lord told him, "I am sending you to them to open their eyes and turn them from darkness to light, and from the power of Satan to God, so that they may receive forgiveness of sins and a place among those who are sanctified by faith in me" (Acts 26:18). In other words, Paul, the battle is on!

We must understand that in a very real sense Jesus' entire mission here on earth was doing battle with the devil, taking back ground in spiritual warfare, and establishing the kingdom of God on earth. When we pray for the sick, cast out demons and declare the rule of God among men, we are in a cosmic conflict. John declares boldly, "The reason the Son of God appeared was to destroy the works of the devil" (1 John 3:8b). If the church is to make any headway in this world, we too must adopt a warfare worldview.

> Without the twin ministries of healing and deliverance, our preaching that God's kingdom is here and that Satan's dominion is being destroyed is hollow.[64]

Nigeria

In 1989 I visited Nigeria with a team of evangelists from the United States. We were there to preach crusades at the invitation of the Methodist Bishop over the area. We were also starting churches in regions where no churches existed. I saw 5,000 people come to the Lord in a month's time. The people were so hungry for God.

One night we were preaching in the city of Oron. The service lasted five hours. I remember praying the entire time, off the sanctuary in a little "prayer closet." That night an 11-year-old girl manifested evil spirits. We prayed over her, casting out the spirits for the better part of an hour. She was free when we left. No one thought it strange that we would minister deliverance during the service. They understand the spirit realm in the Third World.

Upon returning home to our bunkhouse that night, vultures were perched on the roof—not a good sign. We were in the midst of deep spiritual warfare in a region with witch doctors and devotees of animism. The room was infested with five-inch cockroaches. It took a while to get them all, but I was not about to turn out the lights until they were gone! My partner, Frank Beard, was in one room and I was in the other. Little did I know that he was attacked by a demon spirit and was having the sensation of being strangled during the night! He couldn't even call out for help because his voice would not work. He could barely breathe. It was a terrifying experience.

Finally, after calling on the name of the Lord in his mind and spirit, the demon left. He really thought maybe this was the end, but God delivered him from the dark visitor. I am sure people were praying for us back home during this very time, or we could have been overcome. God is faithful and covers us at all times.

I tell you this to emphasize the fact that we are living in a cosmos where "spiritual beings exist between humanity and God, and whose behavior significantly affect human existence, for better or for worse."[65]

When we see the biblical authors waging war against such things as injustice, greed, oppression, and neglect of the poor, what we really are witnessing is a cosmic war that has engulfed the earth. These unseen forces have as their goal to wreak havoc on earth and diminish and destroy the image of God in man.

This is a cosmic event that extends beyond the temporal realm. Until the church understands this, she will be at a disadvantage. A few years ago, I heard Jack Hayford make this statement at a training event in Akron: "Every day hell is at its worst, trying to accomplish its most. There is never a nice day in hell. Spiritual warfare is constant. It never lets up, and neither can you."

Here is the "rub" for the church in America. Our Western materialistic worldview has dismissed all of this business about an invisible personification of evil and instead, it has turned into an intellectual puzzle, where misguided people make wrong choices. It is thought if only a person's educational level could be improved, and their environment could change, then much of the dark side would just disappear.

Furthermore, what is really scary is that we are totally out of touch with the rest of the cultures of the world. Our myopic view of the supernatural is actually working to keep us in bondage to spiritual powers. Most cultures outside of Western civilization currently have a working knowledge of this cosmic battle and have developed religious systems to deal with its challenge. In fact, only Western Christianity's intellectual approach views this cosmic battle (that hoists dark and forbidding things upon the people of the earth) as nothing more than "ignorant, primitive superstition."[66]

All this became very apparent on March 16, 2001, when I was watching an interview on Book TV with Rabbi Harold Kushner, author of the best-selling *Why Bad Things Happen to Good People*. The basic argument of the book is that pain and suffering are all a part of the good purposes of God, and that our basic dilemma is not the existence of evil powers and beings, but bad choices. Then he made this statement: "Good people do good things because they are good; good people do bad things because they are human." I would have to disagree on both counts.

The Bible makes it very clear that man is unrighteous to the core. (See Psalm 14:3, Isaiah 53:6, Romans 3:23) Man is not innately good; he is innately flawed and in need of redemption. Subsequently, his "bad things" flow from an unregenerate nature, not from being human (Psalm 1:6, Jeremiah 22:13). Tell the families of the victims of 9/11 that the terrorists were just being "human" in their unfortunate choices. Because of man's sin condition, we desperately need a biblical worldview to navigate the war zone called Planet Earth.

Scripture Is the Bottom Line

I believe the church entering the 21st century must give credence to the plethora of "evidence" concerning Satan and the kingdom of evil as portrayed in the Bible and as experienced in everyday life.

Every day we have a running record of the devastation and havoc plundering our world in the form of the morning newspaper. It's even delivered right to our door. How can any thinking person deny that this planet is under assault? Gregory Boyd says, "The world is a spiritual battle zone, which is why it looks that way!"[67]

The assumption that Satan has illegitimately seized the world and now exercises a controlling influence over it undergirds Jesus' entire ministry. Three times in the Gospel of John, Jesus refers to Satan as the "ruler of this world" (John 12:31, 14:30, 16:11 RSV). He uses the word *archon*,[68] which was used customarily to denote the highest official in a city or region.

When Satan claims that he can give the glory and authority over all the kingdoms of the world to whomever he wants, Jesus does not dispute him (Luke 4:5–6). Apparently the apostles and the rest of the early church recognized this as well. Note these verses:

- 1 John 5:19—"The whole world is under the control of the evil one."
- 2 Corinthians 4:4—"The god of this age has blinded the minds of the unbelievers . . ."
- Ephesians 2:2—Satan is called "the ruler of the kingdom of the air."

We are battling a formidable enemy, and we'd better know the rules of engagement, or we will become a casualty. That is the way it is in war. The good news is that Jesus is able to tie up the strong man. Luke 11:22 says, "But when someone stronger attacks and overpowers him, he takes away the armor in which the man trusted, and divides up the spoils."

The New Testament makes it abundantly clear that Satan and his minions have been defeated by the cross and the resurrection, and one day will be destroyed! (see Colossians 2:15; 1:13, Hebrews 2:14, Revelation 11:15).

Until that time, we are called to live in the tension between the already and the not yet. We live in two worlds—the present physical world, too often defined and bound by physical matter, and the world to come, which shall certainly and eventually be revealed and which lays before us the hope of dwelling with God in majesty and glory forever. F. F. Bruce, a great New Testament scholar, said we are a hybrid people, born of the flesh in one age, but alive in the Spirit in the age to come. Every time someone is healed or forgiven, or an act of goodness transpires, or we sing a hymn and worship, it becomes a foretaste of the world to come.

Yes, there is a militant, radical, warring side of the church, but it is warring for the right reason. We are here to expose oppression, injustice, and darkness in whatever form it may take, and to put the devil on notice that he was defeated at Calvary and he must release the captives. We are warring with the Lion of the tribe of Judah at our side, and we are to lay claim to all that Jesus has purchased with His precious blood.

If you are a born-again believer and Christ is your Lord, all that He has becomes yours. In the New Testament it is known as our inheritance (1 Peter 1:3–4). With it comes healing, deliverance, a renewed mind, and a glorious future. This is the good news we are to announce to the world and celebrate as we live the days of our lives. So, it is no wonder that people respond when we "do the stuff." I have personally seen hundreds of people healed across my ministry—heart disease, cancer, fibromyalgia, broken bones, lengthened legs, and many others.

I was holding a meeting in Cambridge, Ohio, a number of years ago, and when I gave the altar call for healing a man came forward with Crohn's disease. Even though Crohn's is incurable, we prayed. I felt the power go into his body as I prayed. A few nights later he returned to the meeting, confirming a total healing by his physician! Is there anything too difficult for God? (Jeremiah 32:17).

As Gregory Boyd says, "Wherever there is destruction, hatred, apathy, injustice, pain, or hopelessness, whether it concerns God's creation, a structural feature of society or the physical, psychological or spiritual aspect of an individual, we are in word and deed to proclaim to the evil powers that be, 'You are defeated.' "[69]

As the last-days church, we will live prophetically; our lives reflecting the new day that is dawning upon the world. Signs, won-

ders and miracles will be a forerunner to that day. Be sure to know
that Jesus will return for a glorious church proclaiming a glorious
gospel!

The Recovery of the Supernatural

My heart goes out to pastors. I know many clergy who deeply desire
to experience what they read in their Bibles. There just seems to be
an impregnable wall that many cannot seem to get beyond. There
are so many good ideas, so many "church models," and so many
choices. America is drowning in choices. We feel the pressure to
give people what they want, knowing silently in our hearts it is not
always what they need.

We have become so process-oriented in the post-modern
church, so managerial in our style, that we have all but lost the
glory and the supremacy of Jesus in the midst of ministry. What
most of our churches want is a good business administrator, but
what most need is a recovery of the supernatural—all the way from
praying for miracles, to believing in heaven as a real place of existence following death. The time is shorter than we think, and the
world is crying out for authentic lives that are totally surrendered
to God.

I am trusting God for a recovery of the supernatural right in
the sanctuary of your county seat church. God wants to come. Let's
prepare to make Him feel welcome and see the glory of God where
we live. Second Chronicles 16:9 (KJV) is still the plea of the God of
the Bible: "For the eyes of the Lord run to and fro throughout the
whole earth to shew himself strong in the behalf of them whose
heart is perfect toward Him."

Some years ago God gave me this prophetic word on restoration. It came after reading Isaiah 35 and the "Highway of Holiness"
upon which the remnant will walk in the last days. I invite you to
pray over it and claim it for your life and ministry, as the Holy
Spirit contextualizes it where you live. Speaking of the people of
God:

This group will be a healing, refreshing, restoring, remnant church. They will stimulate the relationship that Adam had with God in the beginning. They will know His name; they will love His Word; and they will worship Him in spirit and in truth. And all the earth will take note of them. They will be a chaste generation that will be wrapped in the glory of God, and they will be refreshers to the downtrodden and the poor. They will provide a sign to a lost and sinful generation, and witness to the truth and life of the living God. Kings will come to them for understanding, and the wealth of the wicked will be stored up and placed in the lap of this people. They will be impregnated with supernatural joy, and the pervading presence of their God will consume them in zeal, worship and service.

Maranatha . . . come Lord Jesus!

Chapter 7

The Onus of Amos

One of the mandates on the church entering the 21st century is a full-fledged recovery of the ministry to the poor. The body of Christ is God's network to meet this need. The government cannot do it adequately. Government agencies lack accountability, coordination, and compassion for the poor. "Poverty is a complex phenomenon," says Doug Bandow, "because it has more than one cause. Its causes include not only personal infirmity and imperfect social structures; much poverty also results from poor individual decisions—drug use, criminal activity, premature pregnancy, excessive spending."[70]

Many times government means well, but when dealing with poverty there is much more than money at stake. You just can't throw money at a problem and fix it. Walking with the poor requires mentoring and long-term solutions, and that is the church's domain. We have both a God-given mandate and an infrastructure to excel in this calling. We must keep our eye on the target: human redemption. Addressing poverty is part of the equation. As we launch into this discussion, there is no better place to start than the prophet Amos in the Old Testament.

Who Was Amos?

The prophet Amos lived in the middle of the 8th century before Christ in Tekoa, a community in the hill country of Judah, about ten miles south of Jerusalem. We know precious little about him. We do know God called him from a shepherding background (Amos 7:14ff). Rather than being a day laborer, he probably was a respected man in the community, as a breeder of sheep.

Having begun his ministry with oracles of fire and judgment, Amos spoke to the people of the Northern Kingdom of Israel, with its capital in Samaria. He made his frequent rounds both at the temple at Bethel (7:10–17) and in the marketplace (8:4–5). In addition, the officials of the ruling class were never far from his message of doom (3:9–11; 6:1–3).

As James Mays says in his commentary on Amos, the message Jehovah gave him was no less than to announce the end of Israel. "His oracles are in the form of an announcement of judgment, which is composed of reproach and proclamation of punishment."[71]

What could have possibly caused God to raise up a prophet with a message so matter of fact, so categorical, so final? A message in essence saying I am no longer your God and you are no longer my people; in fact, you are "out of here!" Believe it or not, it was not for sexual immorality, making alliances with heathen nations, or worshipping idols made with hands.

No, it was for denying righteousness and justice to the weak, the poor, and the afflicted of their society. Those who already had three strikes against them were neglected, abused, used, and trampled upon by those who had the power. They were sold into slavery (2:6), disposed (8:6), and exploited (5:11).

The Onus of Amos

Anyone who has studied the Old Testament and the history of Israel knows the special obligation and concern the nation had to protect the weak and the poor. This national safeguarding of the poor was to be a witness to the nations of the world that Jehovah was a God of a different stripe. After all, their God was a God of compassion and concern. This theme carried through the entire structure of the Old Testament period. Listen to the exhortation to Israel early on:

If there is a poor man among your brothers in any of the towns of the land that the LORD your God is giving you, do not be hardhearted or tightfisted toward your poor brother.

Rather, be openhanded and freely lend him whatever he needs. Be careful not to harbor this wicked thought: 'The seventh year, the year for canceling debts, is near,' so that you do not show ill will toward your needy brother and give him nothing. He may then appeal to the LORD against you, and you will be found guilty of sin.

Give generously to him and do so without a grudging heart; then because of this the LORD your God will bless you in all your work and in everything you put your hand to. There will always be poor people in the land. Therefore I command you to be openhanded toward your brothers and toward the poor and needy in your land (Deuteronomy 15:7–11).

How could this happen to a people who had such a clear mandate? Could it have been about power, privilege, greed, and neglect of the spiritual side of life? These people committed the highest treason of the day—neglect of the poor.

Another prophet a few hundred years later reminded his generation that the indictment over Sodom was not just for sexual immorality. "Now this was the sin of your sister Sodom: She and her daughters were arrogant, overfed, and unconcerned; they did not help the poor and needy" (Ezekiel 16:49).

Amos thundered at the abuse taking place throughout the society. (Read Amos 2:6; 3:9, 15; 4:1; 5:10–13; 6:4–7; 8:4–6). In these Scriptures God exposed a corrupt court system, an arrogant, affluent upper class (as if they were the only ones that mattered), and a corruption in the worship of God, even to the notion that God would help continue their carnage (5:18).

Their greed knew no bounds; their pride over their status and achievement was nauseating to the Lord. Therefore, Amos descended on this repugnant nation and delivered a decree of disaster. An invader will ravish your land (6:14); your defense will be razed (3:11; 5:3); and exile will be your future (6:7; 7:11). The consequence that awaits them will be so dreadful that there is no mention of repentance or reform. This is a "done deal."

A Clarion Call for Today

When we read the Book of Amos we cannot miss his rage at the abuse and neglect of the poor. God's people in every age have been called to minister to this sector of the society, who Jesus said, "you will always have with you." This was the onus of Amos, and it is our continual concern today. The poor will be forever on God's heart; and we, the church, have been given a mandate to help them.

It is inconceivable to think that a fertile ground for the gospel can be maintained if the lives of the people in our communities are diminished. For example, children who go to school hungry and ill clad are at a disadvantage in the learning process. How can we help address these problems? It's not rocket science. Discernment and action are the only two things called for here. The theme comes up continually throughout the Scriptures.

- Psalm 12:5—"Because of the oppression of the weak and the groaning of the needy, I will now arise, says the Lord. I will protect them from those who malign them."
- Proverbs 14:31—"He who oppresses the poor shows contempt for their Maker, but whoever is kind to the needy honors God."
- Proverbs 14:21—"He who despises his neighbor sins, but blessed is he who is kind to the needy."
- Proverbs 28:27—"He who gives to the poor will lack nothing, but he who closes his eyes to them receives many curses."
- Proverbs 31:9—"Speak up and judge fairly; defend the rights of the poor and needy."

Also consider Jeremiah 22:16; Daniel 4:27; Matthew 11:5, 19:21; Mark 14:7; and Luke 6:20. Poverty is a broad subject, as I have said. Continuing in the New Testament, we could review Luke 14, the parable of the great banquet, and Matthew 25 about when feeding and clothing the least of these, doing it unto Christ.

We could read Romans 15 and 2 Corinthians 8–9 which elaborate Paul's model for the sibling churches to remember the Mother Church in Jerusalem and take up offerings for her.

We could review the distribution method in Acts 11:22–30, where the elders and those who have established a worthy track record in channeling funds connect with the poor.

Finally, there is the disturbing question in 1 John 3:17 (RSV), "But if anyone has the world's goods and sees his brother in need, yet closes his heart against him, how does God's love abide in him?"

The Servant Nature and the Poor

I believe if our action toward the poor is going to bear long-term fruit, it must be done with a servant nature. Jesus had very specific things to say about being a servant. (Read Mark 9:35, 10:35–45; Matthew 23:11–12; and John 13:3–17.) It was, after all, His *modus operandi*. It was the thing that completely discombobulated His religious contemporaries. You see, they were looking for a prideful, charismatic, warrior ruler. Instead, they got a kind of vagrant evangelist teaching about love and healing the sick. No wonder they were confused.

However, it really does make sense—this servant nature action model. Think about it. First, it is always relevant in every culture and in every age. Second, it is always needed because there are never enough people with a servant nature to go around. It is counter to human nature.

Did you know that early in our nation's history, the church was largely responsible for operating the hospitals, orphanages, almshouses, rescue missions, hostels, soup kitchens, welfare agencies, schools, and universities? The church was a home to the homeless and a refuge to the rejected. As a result, it had equity with the community.

The church also had authority in the culture because it had earned it. Social scientists have identified a link between social service and social authority. Whoever meets the needs of the people will gain the allegiance of the people. The real authority comes when we serve others and they know we are the real deal. (Read Luke 22:25–27.)

The whole information age with its Internet has swept in a new emphasis on service-oriented business. We live among a generation of people who are so *into* themselves that service-oriented business designed to meet their needs will be greatly successful. The wildly popular online bookstore Amazon.com is one example.

We must realize that servanthood is first an attitude and then an action. It's not about us; it's about them. This became the currency of exchange in the ancient world. To the church in the capital of the Roman Empire, Paul introduces himself as "Paul, a servant of Jesus Christ."

- Peter likewise in 2 Peter 1:1 states, "Simon Peter, a servant of Jesus Christ."
- And Jude, the brother of Jesus, "Jude, a servant of Jesus Christ" (v. 1).
- Finally, John the disciple who was closest to Jesus, in the Book of Revelation states that the great vision was made known to "his servant, John" (Revelation 1:1).

If we are going to "major in the majors," we must master the development of a servant nature. As Doug Stringer says in his book, "Men reach for thrones to build their own kingdoms; Jesus reached for a towel to wash men's feet. We must have a servant's heart toward each other and toward this generation."[72]

God is holding up a mirror to the church in this hour and asking, "Why don't you look more like Jesus?"

The Stewardship of Life

In tandem with the servant nature is the area of the stewardship of our resources. Generally speaking, we simply must live smarter than we have been. As Christians, we constantly live with a view to our mission and purpose. We do not have the luxury of living any old way we want. We are called to live disciplined lives, so that when the time comes to give, we have something to offer.

There is no greater example than John Wesley. He actually had a program to lift up his generation into a position to live, with some left over. And remember, 18th century England was very poor. He lived by three simple phrases: earn all you can, save all you can, give all you can. Let's look at them in more detail.

Earn All You Can

Earn all you can, while acknowledging that some ways of making money are not acceptable. Wesley uses the phrase "the sweat of our brow" to say that we are all going to have to bite the bullet and do an honest day's work for an honest day's wage.

By the way, in Wesley's contemporary England, the royalty did not work. They felt they were exempt from earning their bread by the sweat of their brow. There are few things that give a person more self-worth than employment. God put us all here to do something, and it is sad when we fail to relate that to Monday through Friday.

Save All You Can

Wesley was not talking about saving money in IRA's as we do today; however, if anyone had the capacity to be wealthy it was Wesley. Millions of dollars went through his hands. After all, he was highly educated, highly gifted, and blessed with an unusual anointing of the Spirit. He could have had it all, but he refused.

He was talking about living as frugally as you can and only buying what you need. Who among us does that? Not me! This is really a lifestyle issue, not a financial issue. We all will give an account for what we have done with what we have—a chilling prospect.

Give All You Can

When Wesley was at Oxford he only needed twenty-eight pounds a month to live on; all the rest he gave away. The reason we want to have it is so we can give it. This is obviously not the philosophy of the contemporary world and, I am sorry to say, not much of the church either. But it is in God's heart.

You can't take it with you, but you can send it ahead. Someone has said, "I have never seen a hearse pulling a U-Haul, and I have never seen pockets in a shroud." The Bible says we are stewards, so manage that which the Father has entrusted to us. Wesley would say you are rich if you have more than you need. Ouch, that hurt!

There you have it. Simply put, these are the basics. We have a mandate, a mission, and a modus operandi. Getting these moving in the same direction will cause the church to gain great equity in the community where God has placed us. Perhaps then we can realize Proverbs 11:11, "Through the blessing of the upright a city is exalted, but by the mouth of the wicked it is destroyed."

The Church's One Foundation

In the early 1990s a group of suburban pastors in Columbus, Ohio came together with inner-city pastors and launched a foundation to minister to the poor. With approximately 1,000 churches in Columbus and a population of over a million people at the time, the need to reach out to the poor was evident. The "how to do it" was not.

God gave this group of pastors a New Testament model to make the ministry work effectively. The basic concept involved an understanding that the church in the inner city needed help to reach the poor. After all, it was the inner-city churches that already identified the needs with the infrastructure and proven track record, but many times lacked adequate resources. On the other side of the equation, it was the suburban churches that had the resources and the personnel, but did not have the wherewithal to get the resources to the needy.

God summoned twelve highly visible, large suburban churches that had built equity with the community in the greater Columbus area, to link up with inner city churches and pastors who had a place—an identity—and a relationship with the people in need. I was one of the founding pastors in the ministry. The ministry was named "The Church's One Foundation."

The concept was very simple and is found in Acts 11:29–30. "The disciples, each according to his ability, decided to provide help for the brothers living in Judea. This they did, sending their gift to the elders by Barnabas and Saul." It is that simple—sending aid by the elders into the hands of those who need it.

We saw the elders as the inner city pastors and "help organizations" who were responsible to evaluate the needs and apply the resources. One Foundation became a bridge between those able to gather resources and those able to distribute resources. One Foundation did not minister to individuals or start any inner-city ministries.

Even though there were differences in doctrine and tradition among the Board of Directors, these things were set aside in order to join together for the effort. The same thing happened during the dedication of Solomon's temple. "Now when the priests came out of the holy place (for all the priests who were present had sanctified themselves, *without regard to their divisions . . .*" (2 Chronicles 5:11 RSV).

As we began to work together, the biblical pattern looked something like this:

- Identify the needs (Deuteronomy 15:7–11; 1 John 3:16–18).
- Gather financial and other resources from those willing to give in various churches (Romans 15:25–26; 2 Corinthians 8:2–4, 9:2–6).
- Use carefully chosen people to "bridge" the resources to the areas of need (2 Corinthians 8:18–24).
- Give the resources to the elders who live with those in need (Acts 11:29–30).
- Produce results: The poor pray for the givers and those in need give glory and thanks to God (2 Corinthians 9:13–15).

Our initial goal was to enlist two hundred churches that would contribute $400 a month. This would generate $80,000 a month—enough to feed 32,000 people in one day.

Conviction and Purpose

The pastors who originally started the ministry of One Foundation came to the understanding that the suburban churches often receive the benefits of the city, while ignoring the problems of the city. We realized that Columbus was our city, and that we are a part of something larger than just our individual churches. Our brothers and sisters in the inner city regularly deal with the problems of drug abuse and alcohol addiction, violence, single-parent families, pregnant teens, and unemployment. Linking the needs to the resources began to have an impact in the city.

For example, one of the inner-city board member churches had an effective urban renewal network called Diversified Community Services (DCS). The Community Properties Division of DCS had entered into a program with HUD, whereby the church was able to lease vacant houses in the neighborhood for $1 a year. These were FHA-repossessed houses. They would then put between $3,000 and $10,000 into the homes to make them livable.

For a three-year period, a homeless family was placed in one of these homes. Through the help of an action-based community program of rehabilitation, they were able to learn how to care for and live in the house.

At the end of three years, the house was sold to the family on land contract for half the market value. The money generated from these sales was then recirculated into the fund to repeat the process. The only things the family had to pay for during the three-year period were utilities and insurance.

One Foundation would go in and help rehab the houses and provide front monies for the investment. One home worth $46,000 was completely renovated for $10,000. That is redemption of resources! People were taken off the street, given skills they never had before, and then were able to help in the restoration of the community.

I believe this pattern could be multiplied all across the nation. We could see our inner cities come alive with hope and faith in a process that involves accountability and courage. This process also allows the body of Christ to link together and take ownership for the community. We can do things the government can never do and do them more effectively.

As James Robison says, "Why don't we find a way for faith-based organizations that change people's lives to effectively use some of the nearly $9 trillion we have thrown at the poor over the past few decades? We could have bought every poor person in America a house and a Lexus with that kind of money."[73] Cooperation and co-laboring build unity and trust among the pastors, and the darkness gives way to the light of the gospel and the presence of the Lord.

Pregnant with Compassion Ministries

Today my church continues to be involved with ministries to the poor. One Foundation eventually evolved into a secondary ministry called Columbus Leadership Foundation. This ministry took a totally different direction, and we were led to switch our allegiance elsewhere.

A few years ago one of our elders had a dramatic vision from the Lord, encouraging us to do more as a local church in the area of helping the poor. This vision was very specific and caused many in our fellowship to take a serious look at our ministries to the poor. Some people who were formerly involved with compassion ministries had backed off and other ministries had lost the vision. It was a time to reinvest, even though we have always had some outreach intact. Reevaluation and redirection are constant processes that every church goes through. God always seems to be changing things in order to keep us fresh.

Following a concerted time of prayer and introspection, we took the vision to the entire congregation. Conviction came upon the entire house. The Lord led us to do a congregational survey on ministry to the poor. No church can do everything, so we must have direction from the Lord. We passed out the survey over a series of Sunday mornings. As a result of the survey, nine general areas of need were identified. Each of the nine areas was assigned to one of our elders and their wives. The nine areas were:

1. The Homeless—Ministry at homeless shelters and clothing for the poor.
2. The Poor—Meals for families in crisis, food pantry, clothing for the poor, Thanksgiving dinners for the needy and others.
3. Prisoners—Ministering to prisoners, halfway houses for prisoners, maintaining a work program for rehabilitated prisoners, and those in recovery.
4. The Elderly—Home visits to shut-ins, not necessarily our own; home maintenance for widows, single mothers, and the elderly.
5. Patients at Hospitals and Nursing Homes—Worship services for hospitals and nursing homes; in-home visitation.
6. Choir and Praise Team—outreach to prisons and nursing facilities.
7. Visitors—"Who's Who" Dinners, outreach to new people in the community.
8. Teen Ministry—Area churches uniting for outreach opportunities, mission trips and concerts.
9. Health Ministry—Parish nurse program.

Later a tenth category was added, called Mentoring Ministry. This has been a great success, reaching out to people with personal problems and dysfunctions. Following the direction from the Lord, we plugged into ministries of compassion with renewed vitality and joy. God has blessed us in this effort and real needs are being met by an army of compassion, mobilized with purpose. May the name of the Lord be praised!

Keeping Our Eye on the Mark

As we look at the issues of helping the poor, it can become an overwhelming task. The needs are very great, and the effort will never stop this side of glory. In America, the middle class is shrinking and the disparity between the rich and the poor is widening. However, we must remember that the poor are a special concern to the heart of our God, and therefore to us. As we seek the face of God, revelation will come to us and ministry will flow to the poor. The key is we must be willing.

I leave you with the words of Edward Everett Hale, a noted poet and one-time chaplain of the U.S. Senate. He said, "I am only one—but still I am one. I cannot do everything, but still I can do something. And because I cannot do everything, I will not refuse to do the something that I can do."[74]

Chapter 8

The Land of More Than Enough

Sometimes God does outrageous things. Should we be surprised? If the church could ever get a hold on how phenomenal God really is, it would catch on fire. Shame on us for making God a ritualistic tutor who follows our pattern of human experience, being squeezed into a human mindset. His ways are higher than our ways, and His thoughts than our thoughts. I believe the 21st century church will again discover the power and glory of the God of the Bible.

We were just beginning our second major building program under my ministry at Trinity Church when a man walked into my office one day, wanting to conduct a survey of our land. I was busy with a daily ministry load and told my secretary to take care of it. Little did I know that "it" would later prove to be an outrageous thing that God did.

For the next several months the company which this man represented, Enveron (not to be confused with the scandalous Enron), began taking seismic impressions all along State Route 204, where our church is located, in Northern Violet Township, Fairfield County, Ohio. This included our new church property across the road from the old church where we were building a new $1.7 million church complex.

About nine months later in the summer of 1995, officials from the company wanted to address our administrative board. We, of course, said yes, and they proceeded to tell us that they had completed their seismic impression tests and they thought they had located a substantial deposit of natural gas directly under our new church. I thought to myself, if you have to tear the church down to

get to it, forget it. I am not going through this again. We had just
built a new church and a new house, both in the same year, and I
was at the end of my building mode patience.

Enveron wanted the mineral rights to drill. We said, sure—go
ahead. After all, they would do all the work and we would get 12.5
cents of every dollar. Now, I have had no training in Wall Street eco-
nomics, but I knew this was a good investment. It just happened that
the church was located on the edge of a geological formation known
as the Rose Run, with a history of oil and natural gas deposits.

The drilling began in May of 1996. However, representatives
from the company were surprised when a "yellow smoke came
pouring out of the drill equipment. The yellow smoke indicated oil
lay beneath the surface, not natural gas."[75]

Actually, it turned out there were both gas and oil—and in
abundance. The oil, which proved to be high quality crude, came
flowing at the rate of two hundred barrels a day. They actually had
to slow down the flow, because they could not handle the rate. The
first check from the oil company to our church was $10,000. I
thought, wow! This really is the real deal!

I believe this testimony reflects an eternal truth that the church
in America needs to capture in order to fuel the fire. That truth is
that the God we serve is the God of More Than Enough. Ancient Israel discovered this truth, yet not without considerable pain. Let's
pause and consider their experience. Paul tells us in 1 Corinthians
10:6 that we should learn from the experience of the Israelites.

The Land of Not Enough

Actually, three different stages shadowed the people of Israel in
their journey to the Promised Land. The first stage was what I call
the Land of Not Enough. In Exodus 5 we have a picture of Israel
under the yoke of oppression. The Scripture states:

> That same day Pharaoh gave this order to the slave drivers
> and foremen in charge of the people. You are no longer to
> supply the people with straw for making bricks; let them go

and gather their own straw. But require them to make the same number of bricks as before; don't reduce the quota. They are lazy; that is why they are crying out, "Let us go and sacrifice to our God." Make the work harder for the men so that they keep working and pay no attention to lies. (Exodus 5:6–9)

Life was hard for Israel in Egypt. They had been there for over four hundred years. They lived so long in the Land of Not Enough that they didn't know any other way. They had become accustomed to the Land of Not Enough. They just accepted it as their plight in life and went about their way. One day God sent on the scene a voice, seemingly out of nowhere, yet it was a voice from some-where—a haunting voice—a voice they had known, but had lost contact with long ago. This time it came in the person of Moses, the servant of God.

Moses began to lift up the God of Israel and cry out for deliver-ance for His people. He told Pharaoh, "Let my people go." After a number of plague experiences, the Israelite people began to get some hope. They began to look to this deliverer. A heavenly deposit was being made and Pharaoh was getting concerned. So, he put on the pressure to dissuade them from this voice by making them gather their own straw and yet turn out the same quota of bricks per day. That was next to impossible. With that decision they were headed for a breaking point, and God was about to make history that is still observed by devout Jews nearly four thousand years later. It's called Passover.

Parallels in the Church

Far too many people in the church today live in the Land of Not Enough. There seems never to be enough money at the end of the month, never enough strength at the end of the day, never enough hope at the end of the trial. It seems like there is just never enough. There is not enough time, not enough energy, not enough experi-ence.

Perhaps all of us have gone through this land at some point in life. Journeying through it is one thing, but living there is something else. However, there are some positive things we can learn from the Land of Not Enough. We know to look to something greater than ourselves. We know that in our own strength we cannot make it. Our own gifts and intellect are just not enough to cope with life. We must find a better way . . . but where? How?

I have seen many pastors and churches settle into the Land of Not Enough, and actually resign themselves to the lack of hope for any change. Pastors can settle into the routine of "pay the rent" ministry, which some have called maintenance ministry. They do what they have to do to barely keep things chugging along, try to keep as many people happy as possible, never knowing the abundance that lies just beyond the threshold of God's promises. Yet there remains a Promised Land for all of God's children.

The Land of Just Enough

In Exodus 6:4 the story continues in the Land of Just Enough. The Israelites have been supernaturally delivered from the hand of Pharaoh and brought into the wilderness to worship Jehovah. God says, "I know you are hungry, and I understand that you have to eat because I created you that way. I don't expect you to live out in the middle of the desert without anything to eat. I am going to provide for you." Oh, if the church in this hour could learn that one lesson—what glory would fall!

So the Lord said to Moses: "The people are to go out each day and gather enough (manna) for that day. In this way I will test them and see if they will follow my instructions. On the sixth day they are to prepare what they bring in, and that is to be twice as much as they gather on the other days" (Exodus 16:4, 5).

The people went out each morning and gathered manna which fell from the sky, so they could eat their daily portion. It was never meant to remain a be-all/end-all. It was a kind of stepping stone. Their destiny was still ahead.

I know many even today who live in the Land of Just Enough. It is better than the Land of Not Enough, but it is not God's best. Linda and I have lived in the Land of Just Enough, but we "rented," we didn't "buy" because we knew there was a greater destination. God knows all of our needs, and He has not forgotten about His children.

Even as dark and chaotic as things are today, God has not forgotten His church. He will provide for His people right up to the end. In all of this I am not just talking about physical or material needs. The American church is already by far the richest in the world in that category.

No, I am talking about the wherewithal to do and accomplish the will of God in ministry that will punch a hole in the darkness and make a difference in the community where God has placed us. To live between the "already" and the "not yet"—the "already" of Christ's death and resurrection power, and the "not yet" of His eternal consummation and reordering of all things according to His will. Between those two realities Christ is calling this world to Himself, and His voice is the church. God had more for Israel than Just Enough, and He has more for us as well.

The Land of More Than Enough

Actually Israel could have arrived in the Land of More Than Enough much earlier than they did. However, because of rebellion, worship and trust in idols, and reliance on themselves, the process was lengthened. The price paid for sin and rebellion was the loss of an entire generation from the destination of God. Finally, after forty years of wandering in the wilderness and standing at the threshold of a new chapter in their history, Israel took a peek at the Land of More Than Enough. It was indescribable. Hear the report of the Lord:

> Observe the commands of the LORD your God, walking in his way and revering him. For the LORD your God is bringing you into a good land—a land with streams and pools of water, with springs flowing in the valleys and hills; a land

with wheat and barley, vines and fig trees, pomegranates, olive oil and honey; a land where bread will not be scarce and you will lack nothing; a land where the rocks are iron and you can dig copper out of the hills (Deuteronomy 8:6–9).

The search party sent to spy out the land verified all of these things (Numbers 13:27). It was an amazing opportunity, almost too good to be true, but they had to step out of their comfort zone to get there. They had to step into the zone of faith and believe that God would deliver this land to them. That began with the conquest of Jericho. Jericho was the tithe on the promise. It was the firstfruits of the campaign. God said: you give me Jericho, and I will give you the Land of More Than Enough.

As I mentioned previously, in 1984, just three years after a major renovation of our one-hundred-year-old church, the Lord gave us an opportunity to buy thirty acres of land across the road for future development. Some members said, "Thirty acres—what on earth are we going to do with that much land?" It all depends on one's vision. Actually, we could have had seventy acres, which is what was available. It just depends on how big our vision is. That land is now selling for $60,000 an acre. We purchased thirty acres on land contract at $3,000 an acre and paid it off over and above our budget in a one-year period. It was a stretch, but we accomplished it. We did not know then that we would be sitting on a huge oil deposit.

The Principle of Firstfruits

Israel attacked Jericho and leveled the city. God was with them, as He said He would be. "Then they burned the whole city and everything in it, but they put the silver and the gold and the articles of bronze and iron into the treasury of the Lord's house" (Joshua 6:24).

God is asking the church today to give Him the firstfruits of our lives. An obedient church will be a glorious church. It was true four thousand years ago, and it is true today. The world is waiting and watching to see a church that walks in moral cohesion. That means our walk lines up with our talk. The lack of moral cohesion has destroyed many a church and pastor. There is a better way, and it is there for the 21st century church to claim as its own.

I believe God is asking His church for a demonstration of the firstfruits principle across the board. When we release the tithe to the Lord, God releases a blessing to the church. He has ways to bless us beyond our understanding or experience. Scripture says, "Honor the Lord with your wealth, with the firstfruits of all your crops; then your barns will be filled to overflowing, and your vats will brim over with new wine" (Proverbs 3:9–10).

The church I pastor has always been a giving, missionary church. We have deliberately had a plan to bless the body of Christ and the community at large. Each year we give thousands of dollars away to people in need. In addition, we are part of a citywide coalition of churches that blesses the city regularly. We have discovered "give and it shall be given to you" (Luke 6:38). God has brought us into the Land of More Than Enough. He can bring you there too.

One day I asked the project manager on the well site how long the oil had been down there. He said two hundred million years. I thought, God you are just too much. You have saved this oil reserve for us at a time when we really needed it. Who would have thought of it? After all, this is not Texas; it's central Ohio, for Pete's sake!

If that is not enough, the land where the wellhead is located was purchased just a few years earlier and was not a part of the original thirty-acre acquisition. It had just become available almost out of the blue from a five-acre plot that was divided in half next to our property. By the way, the oil well is still pumping as I write this book, almost five years beyond its original projection.

A Final Challenge

The apostle Paul reminds us, "He who supplies seed to the sower and bread for food will also supply and increase your store of seed and will enlarge the harvest of your righteousness. You will be made rich in every way so that you can be generous on every occasion, and through us your generosity will result in thanksgiving to God" (2 Corinthians 9:10–11).

I want to challenge every pastor in America to hold out for the Land of More Than Enough. I have no idea how God intends to bless you along the journey. I only know that God will bless us, because He has blessed us in the knowledge and life of Jesus available to every born-again servant of God.

Peter reminds us, "His divine power has given us everything we need for life and godliness through our knowledge of him who called us by his own glory and goodness" (2 Peter 1:3). There is no lack in God, only a lack of understanding and a lack of will and perseverance in us. God stands ready to demonstrate how wonderfully great He remains.

I believe we are living at the precipice of the church's grandest hour. The world is waiting "to see" a demonstration of the grace and power of God's abundance. Are we going to be the church that will let Him have His way? He really is the God of More Than Enough.

Chapter 9

Walking the Tightrope of Cultural Accommodation

One of the breathtaking natural wonders of the world, and perhaps one of the most visited, (twelve million tourists a year) is Niagara Falls. The mighty Niagara River plunges over a cliff of dolomite and shale at the tune of 600,000 gallons per second. Twenty percent of the world's fresh water lies in the Great Lakes and most of it flows over the falls. It is the second largest waterfall on the planet, next to Victoria Falls in southern Africa.[76]

In 1850, a world famous acrobat, Jean Francois Gravalet, became famous in the U.S. for crossing Niagara Falls on a tightrope 1,100 feet long and 160 feet above the water. Even though he was an accomplished acrobat, it made the journey no less dangerous. One wrong move and he could have plunged to his death in the icy waters below.[77]

This story reminds me of the church at the end of the 20th century. She has twenty centuries behind her and is an accomplished force on the world scene. Nevertheless, she is walking a tightrope over an abyss of an "embedded secular culture," where strategic wrong moves could mean disaster. The pity in all of this is that the church could be flying over the abyss on the wings of eagles, soaring with freedom and purpose on the wings of the Lord of history. Instead, she has chosen another mode of access across the divide, which threatens to compromise all that she has to offer. This remains my observation over thirty years of ministry, and my burden.

121

The church of our day, particularly in the Western world, is in a life-and-death struggle with the forces of evil; and it appears the evil has gained the upper hand. As I try to identify some of the delusion that has come upon the church in these difficult times, I am also aware that history is hurtling toward a great and glorious conclusion, wherein the "kingdoms of this world will become the kingdom of our Lord and of His Christ." At the end, our God not only will have the upper hand, He will have the *only* hand. However, before we get there we have some rough water to navigate.

Measuring the American Church

As we consider the cultural deterioration of our day and the church's complicity in it, I want us to think about the whole idea of measuring in Scripture. I believe God is measuring the American church in this hour, and she is found wanting.

In Hebrew society the emphasis on the accuracy of weights and measurements in commercial, ethical, and legal life was basic to the idea of justice and righteousness. In fact, weights and measures were terms used in the Bible to ascribe or determine the *value of a thing*. It was the Levites who had official responsibility over all measures of quantity and size (1 Chronicles 23:29).

In addition, Scriptures that emphasize the importance of just balances are found in Leviticus 19:35, Deuteronomy 25:13ff, and Ezekiel 45:9–11. The prophet Micah said, "Am I still to forget, O wicked house, your ill-gotten treasures and the short ephah, which is accursed? Shall I acquit a man with dishonest scales, with a bag of false weights?" (see Micah 6:10–12).

In Zechariah 2:1, God is seen measuring for the purpose of restoration. He determined the time of exile to be coming to an end, and the rebuilding of the temple of Zerubbabel to signal the beginning. In 2 Kings 21:13–15, God is measuring for judgment:

> I will stretch out over Jerusalem the measuring line used against Samaria and the plumb line used against the house of Ahab. I will wipe out Jerusalem as one wipes a dish, wip-

ing it and turning it upside down. I will forsake the remnant of my inheritance and hand them over to their enemies. They will be looted and plundered by all their foes, because they have done evil in my eyes and have provoked me to anger from the day their forefathers came out of Egypt until this day.

The measuring line and the plumb line were symbols of God's action in testing the lives of men and women. Jehovah is the master builder and He is coming to inspect His work force—the church. We saw earlier that under the prophet Amos, He had authority to do this and He still has authority to do it today. If there ever was a nation that was given all the necessary raw materials to build a just and good society, it was America.

America is, and has been, a blessed nation; but we are losing ground fast. History's infallible rule, the plumb line, will disclose her deviations. This plumb line is the rule—the law, the Word of God—the custodian of which is the church of Jesus Christ. In the last half of the 20th century, the church has witnessed the greatest single demise of our culture in the history of the nation. Now the fruit is coming home. Many are asking, is it too late for reform?

The Great Disruption

Right before the close of the 20th century, sociologist Francis Fukuyama wrote a book entitled *The Great Disruption,* where he analyzes the trends and consequences of the 1960s Cultural Revolution. In his presentation he contends: "The liberation movements that have sought to free individuals from the constraints of many traditional and social norms and moral rules" have had a detrimental effect on our entire democracy. He continues: "As people soon discovered, there were serious problems with a culture of unbridled individualism, where the breaking of rules becomes, in a sense, the only remaining rule."[78]

My contention is that this culture of unbridled individualism has produced an America far removed from the vision of the

founding fathers, and the reason for this dreadful downfall is because the church of Jesus Christ has been asleep at the switch. As a
result, the church is now engaged in a kind of second American
Civil War. This time it is a cultural war of ideas, philosophies, and
ideologies, with the political and moral divide becoming greater
with each passing month.

"We live in a society in which all transcendent values have been
removed and thus there is no moral standard by which anyone can
say right is right and wrong is wrong. What we live in is, in the
memorable image of Richard Neuhaus, a naked public square."[79]

What used to be a bit controversial is now quite standard fare.
Consider these:

- The family is in disarray and broken through divorce, same
  sex partnerships, and co-habitation. "The percentage of all
  babies born to unmarried teenagers during the years between 1960 and 1992 went from 15 to 70 percent. The rate
  of illegitimate births in the Black community is close to 70
  percent.[80]
- Our schools, by and large, are seedbeds for amorality. The
  leading individual influence on public education in America in the 20th century was, of course, John Dewey. It was
  his "plainly stated view that one of the reasons for public
  schools was to remove the irrational religious influence
  that the children might otherwise retain from their parents."[81]
- Our colleges and universities, for the most part, are run by
  radical left-wing liberals with an agenda. It was not always
  this way. "For more than two hundred years, most of the institutions of higher education in the United States were
  avowedly Christian schools."[82]

  However, radical liberalism standing unopposed by the
  20th century church has won the day. Most people in the
  higher education movement now are purveyors of either
  enlightenment or post-modern ideologies. "The principal
  contribution of the enlightenment was to introduce ration-

alism to philosophy, to press the case that human reason, by observing and deducing, could resolve both moral and factual propositions without the need for resort to divine authority."[83]

- Wall Street has taken a huge hit with its insider trading and its Michael Milken protégés. Corporate America is in freefall with its Enrons and its Arthur Andersens. College and professional athletes are reeling in their transgression of drug abuse, crime, and kickbacks for recruiting. Entertainment is feeling the pinch with its Robert Blakes and its Michael Jacksons. In politics, Bill Clinton put the presidency on the map with his escapades in the Oval Office.

- In TV land, recreational sex is pervasive and is presented as acceptable about six times as often as it is rejected. Homosexuals and prostitutes are shown as victims. Television takes a neutral attitude towards adultery, prostitution, and pornography. It "warns against the dangers of imposing the majority's restrictive sexual morality on these practices."

  However, author Maggie Gallagher says, "A pornographic culture is not one in which pornographic materials are published and distributed. A pornographic culture is one which accepts the ideas about sex on which pornography is based."[84]

- The church in America is faring no better. Virtually every major denomination is in the throes of deciding whether homosexual practice is a legitimate expression of "Biblical Covenant Love." Despite the conclusive evidence in the Bible that it is not, we still cannot seem to figure it out. I have been a delegate to the last three General Conferences of the United Methodist Church (1996–Denver, 2000–Cleveland, and 2004–Pittsburgh), and homosexuality has been the dominant issue at each conference. So far, we remain in the "orthodox" category. The Episcopal Church in America has already crossed the line, with their ordination of Gene Robinson, an openly practicing homosexual, as a bishop of the church.

- The Catholic Church is in one of its deepest controversies in centuries, with the sex-abuse scandals by its priests coming to light in the last few years. To add insult to injury, archbishops around the country have paid hundreds of thousands of dollars in hush money to alleged victims in an attempt to keep it all under wraps. A prominent Catholic priest, Father Richard John Neuhaus, editor of the journal *First Things*, has said concerning the continuing crisis: "The epicenter of the continuing crisis is the simple virtue of fidelity. The crisis is about three things: fidelity, fidelity and fidelity. The fidelity of the Bishops and priests to the teaching of the church and its solemn vows; the fidelity of Bishops in exercising oversight in ensuring obedience to that teaching of the vows; and the fidelity of the lay faithful in holding Bishops and priests accountable."[85]
- The financial scandals of the 1980s and 1990s among prominent evangelical and charismatic leaders around the nation have bred distrust all across the spectrum concerning giving patterns to church and non-profit organizations.
- If all of this isn't enough, Martha Stewart just served six months in a minimum security prison for conspiracy, obstruction of justice, and making false statements. America's homemaker is a criminal! Where are we headed in America?

Moral Collapse and National Security

Some have suggested that our national security could be tied to the moral vacuum in America. "Just after the United States invaded Afghanistan, a series of amusing cartoon panels made the rounds on the Internet. Under the heading, 'What if the Taliban Wins?' were drawings depicting the Statue of Liberty, her face covered with a veil; a giant mosque rising where the World Trade Center stood; and an out-of-work President Bush selling fruit on the street."[86] Hence, the association with Islam.

We may have won the war, but the jury is still out on who will prevail in the battle between democracy and radical Islam. Harvard professor, Samuel Huntington, writing at the midpoint of the 1990s, suggested that the world is divided not so much by geographical boundaries as by religious differences. He said the 21st century will be characterized by a great clash between Islam and the West. "The rivalry of the superpowers is replaced by the clash of civilizations."[87]

What is interesting here is that four of the five largest world religions are also associated with civilizations. They are Christianity, Islam, Hinduism, and Confucianism.[88] Huntington says that Islam will ultimately prevail. We had better hope to God he is wrong.

Charles Krauthammer, writing about this conflict, notes that it is not only about religion, ideology, political power, and territory, but it is also very much about sex and morality. "The jihads claim that wherever freedom travels, especially in America and Europe, it brings sexual license and corruption, decadence, and depravity."[89]

Islamic terrorists don't see themselves as terrorists, but as holy warriors fighting holy wars against decadence. I believe one reason we may be at a distinct disadvantage in this war is that we cannot discern our own moral depravity in the United States. America's increasing decadence is giving aid and comfort to the enemy. When they see news coverage of same-sex couples being married in U.S. cities, we make our kind of freedom abhorrent.

We may very well be on a collision course with history. Is history going to repeat itself? Some years ago Will and Ariel Durant, who wrote the massive *History of Civilization* series, were interviewed on television. They were asked: What is the reason for the great collapse of the great empires of the world such as Rome? The thread that tied them all together was the same—the loss of respect for human life and sexual immorality being accepted as normal.

In twenty-two civilizations that have made up the history of this planet, none have endorsed gay marriage, authorizing it as an acceptable lifestyle. On May 17, 2004, the State of Massachusetts began to issue same-sex marriage licenses as official documents.

I believe the church cannot fail to engage in the cultural wars presently buffeting the nation. Addressing America's moral decline may be a matter of moral conscience as well as national security. God is watching and waiting in the wings. If America continues to reject truth and embrace the lie, God will have to judge this nation.

Judge Bork suggests any one of the following four possibilities could lead to moral and spiritual regeneration, thereby averting God's judgment while presiding over the defeat of modern liberalism. They are: a religious revival, the revival of public discourse about morality, a cataclysmic war, or a deep depression.[90]

I am holding out for the first alternative, but would settle for the second. The bottom line is this: The radical individualism mentioned earlier has, in Judge Bork's words, "brought us to the suburbs of Gomorrah."

Syncretism, Double-Mindedness, and Apathy

As we lunge into the 21st century, the drag of the "Babylonian captivity of modernity"[91] from the 20th century is still very much with us. I am very unsettled that this has happened during my watch in thirty-some years of ministry. Did anyone ever think that we would come to the point in the United States where we would have to vote on whether to keep marriage between a man and a woman? Unfortunately, this seems to be the "status quo." Ronald Reagan said the status quo is Latin for "the mess we are in."

I don't know what the answer is, but I do know that before we see God part the Red Sea, we have to get out of Egypt! What do I mean? The American church has become fat and satisfied, comfortable and complacent. We have lost the vision of what it means to be the church promoting the kingdom of God. We are stuck in the "I go to church mode," but that is no longer going to be sufficient. We must rediscover how to be the church to our culture, and we must do it without compromising the gospel. Let's start by dealing with double-mindedness.

I am always amazed that even though the names and faces change, the problems of mankind remain the same. Double-mindedness and syncretism are problems prevalent in "pewland." These are not new problems. In the Old Testament, the god Moloch, worshipped by the Ammonites, used rituals that involved child sacrifice. This was strictly forbidden in Israel (Leviticus 18:2, 20:1–5).

So why did Solomon set up an altar to Moloch on the Mount of Olives (1 Kings 11:7)? Why did Manasseh establish rituals in the Valley of Hinnom (Jeremiah 7:3, 22, 35)? Why would they ever want to do such things? Politics! St. Augustine defined politics as the attempt to reconcile conflicting human wills. Solomon violated one of the big three sins of Israel—intermarriage. Along with his foreign wife came her foreign gods. The next step: accommodation. The rest is history.

One might also call this kind of betrayal syncretism. The word comes from a Greek root which means "to mix"—an attempt to blend opposite and contradictory tenets into one system to produce union and accord. Mixture dilutes truth and reality, reducing its effectiveness. When a person is only 40 percent or 50 percent clear on how to live, their values and standards will also be unclear, and their lifestyle will be inconsistent.

Author Graham Johnston says, "Post modernity is characterized by rabid syncretism that encourages individuals to pick and choose beliefs. Since matters of faith constitute private truth, one can believe anything or nothing; mix and match elements from the various systems of belief without any apparent difficulty."[92]

In a "post traditional world of increased pluralism, relativism, and tolerance virtually assures a shift of perspective on truth and ontological certainty."[93]

The Barna Surveys

Perhaps this is why George Barna, one of the nation's premier church statisticians, found in a 1997 survey comparing the church to the world on 152 different items, that there was virtually no difference between the two positions of the church and the world. The answers to such questions posed below were almost identical for born-again Christians and non-Christians.

- Have you bought a lottery ticket in the last week?
- Have you been divorced?
- Have you filed a lawsuit against someone in the last year?
- Have you had a session with a professional counselor in the last year?
- Have you taken drugs or medication prescribed for depression in the past year?
- Have you watched a PG-13 or R-rated movie in the past 3 months?
- Have you watched an X-rated movie in the last 3 months?

In most of these questions the respondents were within one or two percentage points of each other.[94]

"The heart of the matter is the scandalous failure to live what we preach. The tragedy is that poll after poll by Gallup and Barna show that evangelicals live just like the world. The disconnect between our biblical beliefs and our practices is heart-rending."[95]

In all of this, there is bound to be some good old-fashioned apathy. Folks are so busy and harried these days that they just do not have time to get "involved" with the great issues of the day. After all, there are kids to get to soccer practice, groceries to pick up, out-of-town meetings to attend, deadlines to meet, bills to pay, and on and on and on.

A guest speaker at our church recently called it "crisis mode living," and far too many of us—if not all of us—have been touched by it in recent days. He said the space between load and limit defines the margins of our lives, and most of us seem to have little or no margin left. Living without margins is living in crisis mode. It becomes an enemy of our destiny.

And so we get caught up in the time crunch while our culture goes down the tubes. As Stephen Carter says, "If we decide that we do not have time to stop and think about right and wrong, then we do not have time to figure out right from wrong, which means that we do not have time to live according to our model of right and wrong, which means, simply put, that we do not have time for lives of integrity. It is fine for Socrates and Augustine to stop and think, to take the time for discernment. What else did they have to do with their lives?"[96]

The time crunch is a classic American phenomenon, but it could be jeopardizing the health of our culture and our lives. Think about it.

A Biblical Worldview

The reason for the similarity of respondents in the Barna surveys is due to the issue of a worldview. "Survey after survey has shown that Americans—including a huge majority of born-again Christians and evangelical Christians—lack a biblical worldview."[97]

What is a worldview? A worldview is a perceptual filter through which one sees life and its opportunities. It is the way one looks at the world and evaluates events, circumstances, and information on a daily basis. The Bible says, "As [a man] thinketh in his heart, so is he" (Prov. 23:7 KJV).

Developing a biblical worldview is tantamount to making choices about what we think and what we allow to penetrate our internal being. We have a responsibility for stewardship of the eye and the mind before Almighty God. As we develop a biblical world-view, we will make deliberate choices in life that line up with the revelation that we have received from the Word of God.

So how does one obtain a biblical worldview? Reading, studying, memorizing, and understanding the Word of God are keys to a biblical worldview. The Bible is God's repository of truth, not only for the believer, but for the entire creation. Jesus claims to have been present in a pre-incarnation state presiding over creation. He also claims to have risen from the dead, have ascended back to the Father, and will return to judge the world. These accomplishments comprise a stellar résumé in anyone's book!

Many people will receive the privilege of living in God's presence in eternity on the basis of their confession of faith in Jesus Christ in this life. The ability to make our faith tangible and meaningful in this life demands that we have a transformed mind and a biblical worldview. With only the relationship to Jesus, you will make it through, but at points you may be clinging to Him for dear life, rather than walking confidently with Him in every experience.

Here are the broad strokes. God created us and everything around us for a purpose. The world and all that is in it is not random. The scientific method established that fact last century. There is birth, life, death, and life-after-death. All these fit into a context, a master plan, if you will. When our life has fulfilled God's purpose, it will end. The Bible says, "Just as man is destined to die once, and after that to face judgment" (Hebrews 9:27). "For everything there is a season, and a time for every matter under heaven; a time to be born, and a time to die." (Ecclesiastes 3:1–2 RSV) As we cooperate with God, we experience our destiny in this life.

George Barna says Jesus had four elements working together that facilitated His worldview. "First, He had a foundation that was clear, reliable, and accessible. Second, He maintained a laser-beam focus on God's will. Third, He evaluated all information and experiences through a filter that produced appropriate choices. Fourth, He acted in faith."[98] This closely supports exactly what I have said about developing a biblical worldview.

Like our ancestors, we have had a difficult time in the church keeping the water un-muddied, because we have failed to develop in our people a biblical worldview. We have settled for a few hours on Sunday morning and some spare change in the offering plates. "The average church member (from across the denominations) today gives about 2.6 percent of his or her income—a quarter of a tithe—to the church."[99] At the end of the day, in far too many of our churches, we have little to show for our discipleship. Elijah was right—we must choose whom we will serve every day we live.

Paul reminds us in 1 Corinthians 10:21, "You cannot drink the cup of the Lord and the cup of demons, too; you cannot have a part in both the Lord's table and the table of demons." If we are to slay syncretism and defeat double-mindedness, we must return to the supremacy of the Lord Jesus Christ and the Holy Scriptures as our refuge. Only then can we say with the psalmist: "I hate double-minded men, but I love thy law" (Psalm 119:113 RSV).

The Challenge of Post-Modernism

Historians and sociologists tell us that the deterioration of the modern era (from the 1960s through the 1990s) led to a cultural downward spiral into what is now called post-modern thinking. Post-modernity "refers to a broad range of late twentieth-century intellectual and cultural movements in the fine arts, architecture, communications, media, politics, the social sciences, literary theory and hermeneutics, and philosophy that perhaps are connected more by what they reject than by what they affirm."[100]

To be specific, "post modernity involves the rejection of the assumption that reason leads us to ever-expanding knowledge of reality and that dramatic developments in science and technology result in ever-greater progress for humankind."[101] So much for the enlightenment! However, from the Christian perspective, it amounts to a way of processing the world by negating three thousand years of Judeo-Christian history and thinking. The only rules in a post-modern world are the ones you make up as you go.

Truth, in any objective or absolute sense, no longer exists. At best, truth is relative—a matter of interpretation—and it all depends on the perspective. At worst, truth is "socially constructed, merely a matter of human convention."[102]

Guinness gives us a perfect example of the transition to post-modern thinking with the illustration of the baseball umpires. Three umpires debate their philosophies of umpiring:

> "There's balls and there's strikes," says the first, "and I call them the way they are."
>
> "No, explains the second umpire. "That's arrogant. There's balls and there's strikes, and I call them the way I see it."
>
> "That's no better," said the third umpire. "Why beat around the bush? Why not be realistic about what we do? There's balls and there's strikes, and there ain't nothing 'til I call them."

The first represents the traditional view of truth—objective, independent of the mind of the person. The second speaks of moderate relativism, truth as each person sees it. It allows for interpretation. The third expresses radical relativism or post-modern position. Truth is not to be discovered, but created by us.[103]

Since Western democracies have built their institutions and their way of life on the Judeo-Christian understanding of the world, we have in effect another "clash of cultures." The very idea of truth is so basic to freedom and democracy that the entire society stands in jeopardy when it is diminished or disregarded. Without truth there is no freedom.

Since the world has grown from "Twenty democracies to 145 democracies since 1945," there must be some enduring attraction to this form of government.[104] Everyone benefits from the foundation of truth in a free society—teenagers as well as teachers, mothers as well as judges, cab drivers as well as school janitors.

The church of Jesus Christ also stands to lose everything when truth takes a back seat. Truth is the secret to living free. Jesus told His disciples on one occasion, "You will know the truth and the truth will set you free" (John 8:32). Since truth is not up for negotiation, the challenge becomes acute to "package" truth to a generation that applauds everything but absolutes.

The seeker-friendly movement within the church growth, program-oriented world has gained tremendous momentum in recent years. In order to reach the post-moderns, the church orchestrates a "dumbing down" of the Christian presentation, even to the point of removing all Christian symbols from buildings. The presentation is veiled in a slick consumer package that appeals to the emotion rather than to the intellect.

In many cases, the truth of the gospel takes a back seat to appeal and technique. "The principle flaw in the seeker-centric model is that it leaves us to wonder how sinners should be sought. Do we draw them or does God?"[105]

"Audiences are frequently given what they want rather than what they need. Modern day evangelists no longer need theological polish or moral content, but they must be able to sell."[106] "The dilemma is that this person-intensive solution becomes seductive. Once someone focuses on you, on your needs, and makes you the center of attention, it's hard to give that up."[107]

So, as we navigate our way through this world of embedded secularization and post-modernity, the parade goes on. The quest for information, ideas, applications, and solutions to man's interminable dilemma continues to press the church to the wall. In many places the church is broken and needs fixing.

"Many years ago, Dean Inge of St. Paul's Cathedral in London, remarked in words that could be the epitaph for many trendy church leaders, 'He who marries the spirit of the age soon becomes a widower.'"[108] We can curse the darkness all day long, or we can light a candle and allow the timeless message of God's love to penetrate even the most resistant of places.

I conclude this chapter with the words of Rabbi Daniel Lapin, scholar and president of Toward Tradition, a national forum speaking to issues that harm families, erode wealth, and divide the nation. He said at a recent national pastors' briefing:

> America is a great ship and there are some aboard determined to drill holes in the hull. The nation is a living organism and the distinction that keeps her alive is Christianity. In fact, Judaism's life belt is America's Bible belt. And what we need at this time in our national journey is a return to a fiercely fervent Christianity in America.[109]

May his words be prophetic, and may the church rise to her destiny in this crucial hour!

Chapter 10

The Worldwide Outpouring and the Future of American Christianity

The prophet Habakkuk lived in a time not all that different from ours. He lived in times when God was moving powerfully—so powerfully that even God declared that if He told them what He was doing, they would not believe Him (Habakkuk 1:5).

Their culture, like ours, reflected much diversity with respect to religious conviction. For instance, the stark reality was that some men trusted in dumb objects and idols made by hands. Other men trusted in the living God, revealed through the supernatural manifestations corporately received by Israel (Habakkuk 2:18–19).

Habakkuk had a revelation of the greatness of his God, while his culture slid interminably into a chasm of darkness and judgment. Many times, we who believe in the living God find ourselves in an awkward place; yet it is a good place, because we who walk daily with God become desperate and hungry for His reality in our midst.

As we read through Habakkuk, we realize that God is preparing a firestorm from the North—the Chaldeans (by nature a warring and ruthless people)—to plunder Israel. Actually, judgment becomes a familiar theme in all of the prophets. Israel had become a rebellious and disobedient people. The prophets were sent to warn and to call for repentance.

In the midst of all this warning and judgment, the prophet is overtaken by the greatness and glory of God (Habakkuk 2:20). The revelation of God's glory causes Habakkuk to yearn for the day when God is exalted in the earth through His covenant people in a way that marks history—with tracks. Habakkuk exclaims, "I have heard the report of thee, and thy work, O LORD, do I fear" (Habakkuk 3:2 RSV). He knew that God had made "tracks in history" before, so he wanted to see it in his day.

History's God Chasers

The yearning to see God manifest His power and glory is indicative of God Chasers. As Tommy Tenney says, "God is just waiting to be caught by someone whose hunger exceeds his grasp."[110] Throughout history, God Chasers have included men, women and children whom the Lord raises up as trumpets to the culture. They are *firebrands* who will not allow their generation to forget that God is still in charge of this planet and of His holy people. They focus on the vindication of His name among the nations of the earth. Regardless of the current culture, these God Chasers maintain a perspective that is born out of the deep experience of revelation wed to endurance.

Habakkuk is a God Chaser. He is honest to acknowledge his complaint (Habakkuk 1:1–4). From his perspective, things are pretty bad, but they are only bad to those who have known a better way. For those caught up in extortion, cheating, and idol worship, it's a way of life. The sins of exploitation become standard fare in a world gone awry. The God Chaser, however, living in the midst of spiritual dissonance, hearkens to a better way. This becomes Habakkuk's journey toward the end of the seventh century BC.

So what does he do? He *stations himself* to hear what God will do (Habakkuk 2:1). The Lord answers him, "Write down the revelation . . . make it plain" (Habakkuk 2:2).

What is this vision that Habakkuk is to write down? It is this: "For the earth will be filled with the knowledge of the glory of the LORD, as the waters cover the sea" (Habakkuk 2:14). We know it is yet in the future because the vision "awaits its time."

As God Chasers we are stationing ourselves to hear what God is saying and doing in our time. I believe God is fulfilling this vision, at least in part, through the 20th century Pentecostal/charismatic outpouring. Let's just touch some of the mountaintops of this 20th century outpouring, to bring us up to date.

Mountaintops and More

The outpouring began with an itinerant evangelist named Charles Parham. The year was 1900, and Parham (who held Methodist, Holiness, and Quaker influences) began a school in Topeka, Kansas, known as Bethel Bible College. "Prayer was the central focus of the school, and the prayer tower atop the mansion was in use twenty-four hours a day, with each resident of the school participating in a prayer vigil."[111]

Three days before New Year's Eve, Parham commissioned the students "to search for objective, biblical evidence whereby a person could know for certain that he or she had truly received the Baptism of the Holy Spirit."[112] They were to study primarily the Book of Acts.

On New Year's Eve, upon returning from a ministry trip, Parham reported, "To my astonishment they all had the same story, that while there were different things occurring when the Pentecostal blessing fell, the indisputable proof on each occasion was that they spoke with other tongues."[113]

Later that night, about eleven o'clock, "Agnes Ozman, a Holiness preacher and student of the school, asked Parham to pray for her to receive the Baptism of the Holy Spirit in the manner they had observed in their study. Humbly, in the name of Jesus, I laid my hand upon her head and prayed. I had scarcely repeated three dozen sentences when a glory fell upon her, a halo seemed to surround her head and face, and she began speaking in the Chinese language, and was unable to speak in English for three days."[114]

Azusa Street

Perhaps the most famous event surrounding this new Baptism of the Holy Spirit was spawned at Azusa Street in downtown Los Angeles, in the spring of 1906. William Seymour, a Black Holiness preacher, was very "caught up" in Parham's teaching on the Baptism of the Holy Spirit. He actually attended a short-term Bible school that Parham had started in Houston, Texas, following a successful preaching campaign during 1905.

Seymour attended the school, but did not receive the coveted experience there. However, he was earnestly seeking God for it. During this time William Seymour received an invitation to move to Los Angeles to pastor a newly formed Holiness congregation. He accepted. His first sermon was from Acts 2:4, the biblical experience of the Baptism of the Holy Spirit. It did not sit well with the congregation, and his first sermon also became his last.[115]

Out of money and forlorn, following a series of events, Seymour finally was taken in by Baptist friends, Richard and Ruth Asberry, who lived at 214 North Bonnie Brae Street in Los Angeles. As Vinson Synan says, "They did not at the time accept Seymour's teachings, but they had heard what had happened and they felt sorry for the stranded preacher."[116]

What happened on April 9, 1906, in the Asberry's home changed the religious face of the 20th century. Seymour had just come from praying for a Mr. Owen Lee for healing. Mr. Lee began "speaking in tongues" as Seymour prayed for him, and evidently received the Baptism of the Holy Spirit. Arriving at the Asberry's home, "He related what had just happened with Edward Lee. This news caused the faith of the people to rise higher than ever before, when suddenly, 'Seymour and seven others fell to the floor in a religious ecstasy, speaking with other tongues.'"[117]

When word of this got out, large numbers of people began showing up at the Asberry's home. Within a week's time they secured new facilities at 312 Azusa Street, and the outpouring began day and night. People hungry for more of God began coming from all across the nation and even around the world. This move of God continued non-stop for about three years. The Baptism of the Holy Spirit was on the map, and no one could stop its movement. The "Fire of God" had come to America, and we would never be the same.

John G. Lake, a prominent preacher of the day, commented on Seymour's experience. "God put such a hunger into that man's heart that when the fire of God came, it glorified him. I do not believe any other man in modern times had a more wonderful deluge of God in his life than God gave that dear fellow, and the glory and power of a real Pentecost swept the world."[118]

Evan Roberts in Wales

About the same time as the Azusa Street experience, God was breaking out in other parts of the world. The amazing Welsh Revival of 1904–1905 became a firestorm of revival that touched the world as well. Evan Roberts had been a miner and a blacksmith in his young years, but his heart was with the church and revival. "For ten or eleven years I have prayed for revival," he wrote to a friend.[119] Following those first dozen years, Roberts prayed for a year with such intensity and agony that his landlord asked him to vacate his room.

At the end of October 1904, Evan Roberts spoke to a group of young people during a Monday night prayer meeting in his village of Loughor. The Holy Spirit convinced them all of Christ, and they dedicated their lives to the Lord. "He began to speak every night to increasing crowds. By the weekend, the church was packed."[120] People were overcome by the power of the Holy Spirit. The following weeks witnessed the revival spreading and consuming thousands of people across several counties. In a matter of a few months, the entire country of Wales found itself in an unusual move of God. "I felt ablaze with the desire to go through the length and breadth of Wales to tell of the Savior."[121]

Inside of a two-year period, "one hundred thousand outsiders were converted, drunkenness was cut in half, many taverns went bankrupt. Crime was so diminished that judges were presented with white gloves signifying there were no cases of murder, assault, rape, or robbery or the like to consider. The police became unemployed in many districts."[122] Many revivals blend into an awakening where the entire culture is brought under its power. Such was the case in Wales.

The Healing Revival of 1946

The healing revivals of the 1940s and 1950s are usually associated with the emergence of one William Branham. Branham was a Baptist minister in Jeffersonville, Indiana. He was a humble man with a simple faith. On May 7, 1946, at 11:00 p.m., following a time of prayer, an angel of the Lord appeared to him.

> Fear not. I am sent from the presence of Almighty God to tell you that your peculiar life and your misunderstood ways have been to indicate that God has sent you to take a gift of divine healing to the people of the world. If you will be sincere, and can get the people to believe you, nothing shall stand before your prayer, not even cancer.[123]

Brother Branham immediately launched into a ministry of healing, with great results. He had a particularly powerful operation in the Word of Knowledge. Others joined in this same flow of ministry. Such names as Oral Roberts, Kenneth Hagin, A. A. Allen, and T. L. Osborn are well known for their emphasis on healing and the miraculous.

By 1956, the healing revival was beginning to wane because of internal strife. Some of the issues were coming from the Pentecostal denominations that many of these people represented. Some of the issues were centered around questionable practices by the evangelists themselves. However, these healing revivals provided an important link between the Pentecostal movement as a whole and the charismatic movement to follow.

The Charismatic Renewal

The April 1960 issue of *Time Magazine* carried a story of an Episcopal priest who announced to his congregation that he had been Baptized in the Holy Spirit and spoke in tongues. Controversy ensued, and he was removed from his church in Van Nuys, California, and transferred to St. Luke's Church in Seattle, Washington. With this event, the charismatic movement began in the denominational world. By 1963, *Christianity Today* had reported that there were 2,000 Episcopalians in Southern California experiencing the phenomenon of speaking in tongues.[124]

With the emergence of Pope John XXIII and the Second Vatican Council (1962–1965), changes were coming for the Roman Catholic Church. The Pope expressed his desire for the dawning of a new Pentecost which he said, "is the hope of our yearning." He also directed the churches to pray that the Holy Spirit would renew His wonders "in this our day as by a new Pentecost."[125]

"In 1967, a group of professors, graduate students, and their wives gathered over the weekend of February 17–19, 1967, in Pittsburgh for the first Catholic Pentecostal prayer meeting on record."[126] In preparation for the event, the participants were asked to read the first four chapters of the Book of Acts and *The Cross and the Switchblade* by David Wilkerson. Meeting at a retreat house on the campus of Duquesne University, the Holy Spirit met these believers with Pentecostal power. Vinson Synan recounts what happened next:

> As these Catholic seekers prayed through to Pentecost, many things familiar to classical Pentecostals began to take place. Some laughed uncontrollably in the Spirit, while one young man rolled across the floor in ecstasy. Shouting praises to the Lord, weeping and speaking in tongues characterized this beginning of the movement in the Catholic Church.[127]

If spaced allowed, we could trace this Pentecostal movement through nearly all the historic denominations from 1960 through 1990. This move of God swept into the denominational world, and many believe rescued the historic churches from both a lack of spiritual vitality and long-standing membership decline.

Historian Mark Noll says in his book, *Turning Points,* "One of the most momentous developments in the twentieth-century history of Christianity must certainly be the emergence of Pentecostalism as a dynamic force around the world."[128] Many believe that without this worldwide outpouring of the spiritual power, the church would have suffocated under the 20th century fascination with rationalism and cultural rebellion.

God Continues to Renew the Church

From these and many other examples, we can see that God is not finished renewing the church. In the last one hundred years we have seen the infusion and importance of spiritual gifts brought back into the life of the worldwide church. Whether you refer to Pentecostal, charismatic, or Third Wave, these have been used by God to restore vital ministry in the world.

So, we have a decision to make in our day and time. Like the prophet Habakkuk, are we going to wed the revelation we have to endurance, and walk in the fullness of the life of Jesus? Or are we going to be casual observers and perhaps miss the glory of God in the 21st century church? Today there are 625 million Pentecostal/charismatic Christians in the world; germinated from a humble prayer meeting on New Year's Eve, 1900, in Topeka, Kansas. The glory of the Lord is beginning to cover the earth as the waters cover the sea. Awesome things are on the horizon, and we all must prepare for them.

The Place of Passion in Contemporary Christianity

At the time of this writing, passion for Jesus is raging all around the world. Nominal Christianity outside the Western world is virtually non-existent. God wants to give the American church passion as she pursues her destiny in Christ. This happens when there is a transaction in our hearts between the God of the universe and our eternal being.

- What makes Abraham radical to obey God?
- What makes Elisha want a double portion?

- What makes Daniel resistant to being brainwashed in captivity?
- What makes Moses covet to share the Glory?
- What makes Mary of Bethany break a vial of pure nard over Jesus?
- What makes Cornelius dare to receive from the Jewish apostle?
- What makes Priscilla and Aquila risk their lives for Paul?

The answer to all of these questions is: *Passion!* God has designed the human soul to be passionate, abandoned, and committed. Many people do not want to pay the price that passion brings to the faith context, so we settle for religion. Religion is what we wind up with when we are no longer willing to pay the price that relationship requires. You can be sure, God wants relationship.

Recently, Nicholas D. Kristof, who writes for the *New York Times*, had a piece in the Op-Ed section of the *Columbus Dispatch*. He was writing about the amazing level of commitment in the church of Africa and Asia. "While I was interviewing villagers along the Zambezi River last Sunday, I met a young man who was setting out for his Pentecostal church at 8:30 a.m. 'The service begins at 2:00 p.m.' he explained, 'but the journey is a five-hour hike each way.'"

Then Mr. Kristof says, "The denominations that are gaining ground tend to be evangelical and especially Pentecostal." Finally, he makes this amazing statement, "On Easter, more Anglicans attended church in Kenya, Nigeria, South Africa, Tanzania, and Uganda—each—than Anglicans and Episcopalians together did in Britain, Canada, and the United States combined."[129] I suspect passion is at the core of this report.

What Ignites Passion?

1. Passion is ignited by the revelation of the knowledge of how much God loves me. He has prepared a place for me in eternity—and He did it in spite of my sin. Some people ask

the question, "If God is a God of love, how could He send anyone to hell?" I would counter, if God is a God of Holiness, how could He send anyone to heaven? The answer is simply, love delivered through grace.

2. The Baptism of the Holy Spirit can ignite passion. Our walk with God takes a significant leap forward with this experience. After all, Jesus told the disciples, don't leave Jerusalem until you receive power from on high (Acts 1:4 and 2:38).

3. Crisis can drive people back to the basics, with passion following close behind. Remember the story of the woman with the issue of blood? (See Mark 5:25–29.)

4. Encountering the supernatural can ignite passion. Read Acts 5:12–15.

5. Actively seeking and asking for more of God in your life will also ignite passion. The Father loves to answer these prayers (Proverbs 3:5–6).

The experience of Mary of Bethany (Mark 14:3; John 12:1–3) provides us with a pristine example of passion unleashed. We encounter her six days before the crucifixion of Jesus, while Jesus is visiting the home of Simon the leper. A dinner is being provided in His honor. Mary is there and is quite enthralled with the person of Jesus. Without wavering, Mary gets up and takes the jar of pure nard (costly perfume) which the wealthy used in the preparation of their dead, and she breaks it over Jesus, anointing His head and feet, and wiping His feet with her hair. Everyone is speechless!

Following a few moments of awkward silence, the angry objections begin. Passion will usually elicit these objections, which are typical of those who like Jesus, but don't really love Him. "It's okay to have an interest, just don't go overboard." Mary's action, however, was just over the top—too radical, wasteful, and lacked rational judgment. (See Mark 14:5; John 12:6.)

There always will be questions when people become passionate for God. Passion may be seen as odd, eccentric, and even unstable. However, God created us to belong to Him. Our relationship is with a real person—one who speaks, guides, encourages, reveals, and corrects (Psalm 119:18).

In this account, Mary of Bethany raises the bar of passionate love for God. This one spontaneous burst of passionate recognition was a picture worth a thousand words. She recognized that Jesus was worthy of all the extravagance that she could lavish on Him. He was worthy of the deepest humiliation she could suffer on His behalf. She would waste her entire life on Him if He would give her the opportunity.

Allow me to suggest that this story shows us that we are to give to God without regard to cost. I believe this is where God has His thumb on the church in America. He wants our passion and worship; the simple giving of our hearts in love and obedience. If we withhold from God the thing He wants the most—our heart/worship—then all the externals mean very little.

It is obvious that Jesus approved of Mary's gesture. Mary was one of the only ones recognizing who Jesus was before the resurrection. Jesus spent a good part of that last week of His life with Mary and Martha. He wanted to be among those who would forego the selfish concerns of rivalry and position. Their house was a sanctuary of affection and rest for the Master. Mike Bickel says, "We either waste our lives in sin and compromise, passivity and the cares of this life, or we waste them on Jesus.

We can waste our lives on serving the devil and end up in a flaming trash heap called hell; or we can waste our lives and our resources on Jesus as Mary did, laying up treasure in heaven where moths and rust cannot corrupt and thieves cannot break in and steal."[130]

I believe a major deterrent to our spiritual growth is pride in our own ability. We think we can handle it; we can figure it out; we can last through the present trouble. In reality, God wants us to fall on our faces before Him, and cast our lives with Him, whatever the cost. Mary's sacrifice was expensive, but she poured it out on Him.

What will it take to bring the American church to humility and desperation for God? Will it take tragedy, calamity, disaster, cancer, bankruptcy, loss of health, loss of employment, divorce, economic collapse, instability, or delinquent children? What will it take to render us helpless in the presence of God?

King David did not worry about pride when he brought the ark of the covenant to Jerusalem. The Scriptures say that he danced with all his might. He needed room to "boogie!" It's going to cost us to boogie with God, but oh, the satisfaction!

The greatest thing is that you don't have to know a lot about God in order to have a lot of God in your life. Most of us did not know beans about our spouse before marriage—not really. We thought we did, but how much we learned in the process of covenant! The church in America is being summoned to passionate covenant with God.

Five Reasons People Became Christians in the Ancient World

Wolfgang Simpson details five reasons why people were drawn to the Christian faith in ancient times. The church in the Western world would be well served to study these five concepts in earnest.

1. **Curiosity**[131]

   The thought here is that humans are by nature a curious lot. They will join secret societies and occult groups with elaborate initiation rites, just to find out what is on the other side. Jesus realized this about human nature, and thereby employed a dual style of communication in dealing with the people. For the general population he spoke in parables (Matthew 13:34), to give them enough to make them hungry, but not too much so as to dull their appetite. Conversely, for those in the inner circle—the committed— He spoke directly. He said, "The knowledge of the secrets of the kingdom of God has been given to you, but to others I speak in parables, so that, though seeing, they may not see; though hearing, they may not understand" (Luke 8:10). If we are the salt of the earth, we are to make folks thirsty.

Perhaps we need to feed people salt before we give them milk or meat. He who has ears to hear, let him hear.

2. **Steadfastness in persecution and martyrdom**[132]

    Brother Simpson says, "The first time that many people in the first centuries set eyes on a real, living Christian was when they saw one die." Because the Christian presented a threat to the gods of the Roman Empire, they were oftentimes martyred for their faith. People would be "gripped" by others who so lovingly and even joyfully went to their deaths for their Savior. This passion was obviously supernatural and attractive to the onlooker. People were fascinated by the level of commitment of the disciples of Jesus. The saying has proved to be true: "The blood of the martyrs is the seed of the church."

3. **Exorcism**[133]

    Exorcism has always tweaked the curiosity and respect of the bystander, not to mention the person being delivered. When Jesus delivered a dumb demoniac in Matthew 9, the Bible says that the crowds marveled, saying, "Never was anything like this seen in Israel" (Matthew 9:33 RSV). In addition, when Jesus delivered the man with an unclean spirit in the synagogue at Capernaum, the people "were all so amazed that they questioned among themselves saying, 'What is this? A new teaching!' With authority he commands even the unclean spirits, and they obey him" (Mark 1:27). Church historians such as Ramsey McMullen, as I mentioned earlier, have documented the profound effect that deliverance had on the entire empire shifting to Christianity.

4. **They had found the way to live.**[134]

    As an early sect, the Christian community was called "The Way." These people had found Jesus, who was "the way, the truth, and the life." They organized their community in such a way as to be available to those who were down and out. They had been taught by the Master that the last shall be first, and he who is greatest in the kingdom is least of all and servant of all. Their communal lifestyle was personally fulfilling and socially productive.

In the Book of Acts we find they held all things in common and if anyone had a material need, the church was there to help supply the need. The "people of the way" would bring their goods and set them at the feet of the apostles for distribution to others in greater need. The love was flowing and people were attracted to their fellowship and warmth. As Robert Webber says, "People come to faith not because they see the logic of the argument, but because they have experienced a welcoming God in a hospitable and loving community."[135]

5. **The teachings and person of Jesus**[136]

Wolfgang Simpson says here, "The church did not preach itself; it preached Christ by promoting His teaching and by living His lifestyle." There was a transparency in the early church that we have all but lost in the modern church. People today are so guarded and suspicious. These early Christians were able to convince others that true conversion began not at the level of belief, but at the level of lifestyle.

Jesus' teachings, especially the Sermon on the Mount, radically displaced the philosophies of the ancient world. There was something almost hypnotic about loving your enemies and praying for those who persecute you. Who could do such things? The Christians could do them. All this became a powerful draw to the average person.

As I muse on these five distinctive features of early Christianity, what impacts me the most is that they can be done in any culture. Unlike the "prosperity gospel" in modern charismatic Christianity, these five injunctions truly hold the power to invade and transform any people of culture. My rule of thumb is: If it cannot be exported and utilized in any culture, it is not true Christianity.

Maybe that is why William H. Lazareth says, "The body of Christ, emulating its divine head, is not essentially an earthly institution with heavenly visions of 'pie in the sky by and by'; it is rather a divine reality that assumes human forms and structures within human history in order to regenerate the present with the future power and purpose of God."[137]

So far, so good, says Phillip Jenkins. "Whatever the value of Christian claims to truth, it cannot be considered as just one religion out of many; it is, and will continue to be, by far the largest in existence."[138]

The Future of American Christianity

The future of Christianity is not in jeopardy, but American Christianity has some days of "soul searching" ahead of her. We can tinker with the process and manipulate the structure while we refurbish the technique of "doing church." However, the bottom line is: Do we embody the transforming power of relationship with the living God through the covenant of Jesus' death and resurrection?

We have a crisis of confidence in the American church, more than a flawed procedure. My experience is that God can use any number of "structures" to serve the purpose of the kingdom. God mostly desires to empower vision and to anoint people to advance His cause in the earth. Jesus said nothing is impossible to him who believes. The American church must become a "believing church" again, and then we will see the church rise to her prophetic destiny.

What does the future hold? Fortunetellers make their living at predicting the future. Wall Street lives and dies on confidence, or lack thereof, concerning future financial developments. The church of Jesus in this world remains confident and alive because she knows the end of the book. As someone has said, "I have read the end of the book, and we win!" However, if the end is not in dispute, the journey to the end may very well be in question, particularly for the Western church.

The culture is definitely in a state of flux, and so is the church. C. Peter Wagner says, "The greatest change in the way of doing church since the Protestant Reformation is taking place before our very eyes."[139] Further, "For four hundred years denominations have constituted the principal traditional model for Protestant Christianity. The church structure in which most of us were raised assumed the validity of denominations without question."[140]

Most people tend to have the feeling that the way we do church now will always be the pattern. Unfortunately, that assumption may be killing the church as we know it. Church prognosticators such as Lyle Schaller, C. Peter Wagner, and George Barna continue to prod the church world with evidence that suggests cataclysmic change is on the horizon.

Back to the Future

Most people measure history from the past to the present. However, the end times church will measure history from the future to the present. This world is on a prophetic timetable. God has spoken certain events into history, and they are as good as if they have happened, even though they have not yet taken place. The end times church will live in anticipation of the glorious fulfillment of the ages via Jesus Christ and the apocalyptic witness of the Bible. This "prophetic destiny" will inform much of the church's witness as we come closer to the end of the age and the final consummation of all things.

Alister E. McGrath, Professor of Historical Theology at the University of Oxford, makes some predictions as we move into the 21st century. He believes the future of Protestant denominations in the West "can only be described in terms of—at best—stagnation, and more likely serious erosion of membership, influence and power."[141]

Professor McGrath continues, "If mainline denominations have a future, it is through renewal movements working within their dwindling ranks. In that the driving force behind such renewal is generally either evangelicalism or the charismatic movement—rather than a specifically denominational agenda or resource—we propose to consider these movements, rather than the mainline denominations, as the future determinants of Christianity."[142] This tends to support my position earlier in this book for the validity of our own Aldersgate Renewal Ministries within United Methodism.

Professor McGrath then goes on to name four segments of Christianity that will prevail in the 21st century. They are Roman Catholicism "which will remain the dominant and most successful form of Christianity in the next century"; Pentecostalism, which embraces white as well as African-American groupings and uses "language and form of communication which enables it to bridge cultural gaps highly effectively"; evangelicalism, with its emphasis on conversion and Biblicism; and finally, Eastern Orthodoxy with its "important role in the preservation of the ethnic identity of communities in the West and in its homelands."

No one knows for sure, yet this information seems to corroborate much of the firsthand experience I have witnessed in my travels and ministry opportunities during the last twenty years throughout the body of Christ. I am very hopeful as we move into the 21st century. In fact, I believe the greatest days of the church lie "just over the next rise."

Chapter 11

Your Latter Shall Be Greater

One can tell a great deal about a person by knowing in what he puts his hope. The Old Testament prophet Haggai had hoped for a "revival of hope" in the post-exilic Hebrew community during the latter part of the sixth century BC. God's chosen people had suffered the greatest humiliation of their history when they were carried off to Babylon in 586 BC. There they were forced to praise their God under artificial circumstances. The psalmist describes their plight:

> By the rivers of Babylon we sat and wept when we remembered Zion. There on the poplars we hung our harps, for there our captors asked us for songs, our tormentors demanded songs of joy; they said, "Sing us one of the songs of Zion!" How can we sing the songs of the LORD while in a foreign land? (See Psalm 137:1–4.)

Bewildered and dismayed, they had no one to blame but themselves. They knew exactly why they were exiled—"But it happened because of the sins of her prophets and the iniquities of her priests, who shed within her the blood of the righteous" (Lamentations 4:13).

Haggai's Commission

Haggai and Zechariah appear on the scene in the year 520 BC, eighteen years after the first wave of people returned to their homeland under the Edict of Cyrus (538 BC). The repatriation of these first Hebrews was not an easy process, as one could imagine. Haggai directed his message to those "leading officials appointed by the Persians to administer the civil and religious affairs of Yehud (Judah and Jerusalem)."[143]

These officials were none other than Zerubbabel, the Governor of the area, and Joshua, the High Priest. It is important to note that Zerubbabel was the grandson of Jehoiachin, the last king to reign in Judah prior to the deportation to Babylon. The same family that presided over Israel's demise would steward her back to a place of usefulness.

God promised a measure of restoration to the weary-laden exiles, but only after they rebuilt the temple. Haggai actually admonished the exiles because they had built their own houses, while neglecting the house of the Lord. It still lay in ruins. "Is it a time for you yourselves to be living in your paneled houses, while this house remains a ruin?" asks Haggai (Haggai 1:4).

This action to repent of their "neglect" and rebuild the temple would release a blessing over Israel which they all coveted—"the presence and the glory of God in their midst again." The problem was that seventy years of captivity caused them to lose their solidarity, their vision, and their hope. Haggai would restore hope.

We must remember, much of Israel's identity surrounded the institution of the temple with its ritual and sacrifice. In the temple, the presence of God dwelt; His glory was on display in the holy of holies. In the temple, the priesthood made sacrifices for the sins of Israel. Further, the temple was "ground zero" for Zion—the place that God referred to as "my holy mountain." The simple fact is, the temple and its worship had become a central focal point for a people religiously distinct in the ancient world.

Haggai's Message

Even though Haggai's time of three months was brief, his message carried a "prophetic punch" that many scholars still see as somewhat eschatological in its reach. I believe it touches even to the 21st century.

I am interested in "Haggai's second major oracle, dated October 17, 520 BC, when the work of construction had been in progress for about a month. In a message of encouragement and a promise of hope for the future, Haggai assures the people that God will manifest His presence among them again. It was the last day of the Feast of Tabernacles, which had been preceded by the Day of Atonement (Yom Kippur)."[144] The prophet delivers these words:

> Speak to Zerubbabel son of Shealtiel, governor of Judah, to Joshua son of Jehozadak, the high priest, and to the remnant of the people. Ask them, "Who of you is left who saw this house in its former glory? How does it look to you now? Does it not seem to you like nothing? But now be strong, O Zerubbabel," declares the LORD. "Be strong, O Joshua son of Jehozadak, the high priest. Be strong, all you people of the land," declares the LORD, "and work. For I am with you," declares the LORD Almighty. "This is what I covenanted with you when you came out of Egypt. And my Spirit remains among you. Do not fear."
>
> This is what the LORD Almighty says: "In a little while I will once more shake the heavens and the earth, the sea and the dry land. I will shake all nations, and the desired of all nations will come, and I will fill this house with glory," says the LORD Almighty. "The silver is mine and the gold is mine," declares the LORD Almighty. "The glory of this present house will be greater than the glory of the former house," says the LORD Almighty. "And in this place I will grant peace," declares the LORD Almighty. (Haggai 2:2–9)

The Blessing of the Obedient

Haggai's prophetic declaration in 2:2–9 opens up a whole new day for the people of Israel. Many believe the phrase, "the latter splendor of this house shall be greater than the former," carries with it prophetic implications for our day as well. In fact, I see two things which come in the wake of this prophetic declaration. They are: restoration and glory. Watch for these in the 21st century church in even greater measure. Let's look at them briefly.

1. Restoration

- God is restoring back to Himself all that was lost in the fall of Adam. This includes the restoration of the *penitent:*

> "Restore to me the joy of your salvation and grant me a willing spirit, to sustain me" (Psalm 51:12).
>
> "I have seen his ways, but I will heal him; I will guide him and restore comfort to him" (Isaiah 57:18).
>
> "Return, faithless people; I will cure you of back-sliding" (Jeremiah 3:22a).

- The restoration of *Israel:*

> "Proclaim further: This is what the LORD Almighty says: 'My towns will again overflow with prosperity, and the LORD will again comfort Zion and choose Jerusalem" (Zechariah 1:17).
>
> "The offerings of Judah and Jerusalem will be acceptable to the LORD, as in days gone by, as in former years" (Malachi 3:4).
>
> "Speak tenderly to Jerusalem, and proclaim to her that her hard service has been completed, that her sin has been paid for, that she has received from the LORD's hand double for all her sins" (Isaiah 40:2).

- The restoration of *Creation:*

> "They will beat their swords into plowshares and their spears into pruning hooks. Nation will not take up sword against nation, nor will they train for war anymore" (Micah 4:3b).
>
> " 'In that day each of you will invite his neighbor to sit under his vine and fig tree,' declares the LORD Almighty" (Zechariah 3:10).

God wants to increase His purpose and His progeny throughout the earth. As we progress in the knowledge and the love of the Lord, increase becomes our inheritance. "God blessed them and said to them, 'Be fruitful and increase in number; fill the earth and subdue it'" (Genesis 1:28a). Increase is the normal projection for the people of God, including the church of our day:

> "The path of the righteous is like the first gleam of dawn, shining even brighter till the full light of day" (Proverbs 4:18).

> "For God, who said, 'Let light shine out of darkness,' made his light shine in our hearts to give us the light of the knowledge of the glory of God in the face of Christ" (2 Corinthians 4:6).

2. Glory

Realizing that Haggai was addressing people during a "high holy day," there must have been extra people in attendance for the occasion. When he asked the question, "Who is left among you that saw this house in its former glory?" there, no doubt, could have been a few. Why bait the crowd with such a question? It seems that the obvious comparison between "the two houses"—the one lying in ruins and the one being assembled—would have had to have been stark.

When comparing the resources available to Solomon (1 Kings 10:27) and the absolute glory of the first temple, there could be no comparison. Solomon had all the best craftsmen, unlimited gold and silver, expensive imported lumber; in fact, the building became the most glorious in the entire ancient world at the time.

In spite of all this, Haggai unleashes this dramatic declaration: "'I will fill this house with splendor,' says the LORD of hosts, 'and the latter splendor of this house shall be greater than the former,' says the LORD of hosts." What could he possibly mean by this declaration?

I believe the real splendor of the temple was not the materials used to adorn the building. The real splendor was the presence and glory of God in the midst of the people's devotion to "the Lord of hosts." When Solomon prayed over the occasion of dedication, by the inspiration of the Holy Spirit, he said, "But will God indeed dwell on earth? Behold, heaven and the highest heaven cannot contain thee; how much less this house which I have built!" (1 Kings 8:27 RSV). However, he also said, "Hearken thou to the supplications of thy servant and of thy people Israel, when they pray toward this place; yea, hear thou in heaven thy dwelling place; and when thou hearest, forgive" (1 Kings 8:30 RSV).

Haggai obviously is declaring something beyond himself, in the best of the prophetic tradition. The issue here is not the temple; it is the glory of God. It was the glory that was the real focal point all through Israel's history. As far back as the Tabernacle, God said, "Let them make me a sanctuary, that I may dwell in their midst" (Exodus 25:8 RSV).

Approximately two hundred years after Solomon's temple, Isaiah encountered this glory and was "undone" in the presence of the Lord. The angel touched his lips with a coal from the altar, and he was declared "forgiven" (Isaiah 6:7). At one point in Israel's history, Samuel declared that the "glory had departed," when the ark of God had been captured by the Philistines (1 Samuel 4:21).

The prophets were always looking for the "greater glory" that was to be revealed in the Messiah of Israel:

"From the west, men will fear the name of the LORD, and from the rising of the sun, they will revere his glory. For he will come like a pent-up flood that the breath of the LORD drives along. The Redeemer will come to Zion, to those in Jacob who repent of their sins," declares the LORD (Isaiah 59:19–20).

Arise, shine, for your light has come, and the glory of the LORD rises upon you (Isaiah 60:1).

These and many other Scriptures are indicative of the new day that will dawn with the revealing of the Messiah. The note in my study Bible concerning Haggai 2:9 says, "This should not be taken as referring to external splendor, for in that respect the temple of

Solomon greatly surpassed this new edifice under construction by Zerubbabel. It refers rather, to the spiritual glory which would be granted when Jesus of Nazareth Himself entered its courts and preached the gospel to Israel in its precincts."[145]

- In conformity with the ancient prophets, when Jesus was born, it was the glory that was on display. John describes it: "We have beheld his glory, glory as of the only Son from the Father" (John 1:14 RSV).
- The angels, along with the shepherds out in the field, declared "Glory to God in the highest" (Luke 2:14 RSV).
- Finally, Simeon, when Jesus was presented to him in the temple "to do for him according to the custom of the law," held the baby Jesus and declared, "A light for revelation to the Gentiles, and for glory to thy people Israel" (Luke 2:32 RSV).

We should be encouraged that this same glory is being revealed all around the world as churches come alive to the presence and power of God in the 21st century. When the glory hits the darkness, Jesus is there "to shine on those living in darkness and in the shadow of death" (Luke 1:79). Sin gives way to light, and transformation is the result. This, then, is the greater splendor spoken of by the prophet Haggai.

Prophetic Pressure Points

As I meditate in the Spirit on Haggai's prophetic word of hope, I feel there are a number of further applications for us from this declaration: "Your latter shall be greater." I will call these *prophetic pressure points* for the 21st century church.

1. Your latter shall be greater because: The Holy Spirit is a resident, not a visitor. Selah! (John 14:16–17)
   This has been the single most important "realized truth" of my Christian walk. Following the Baptism of the Holy

Spirit, the tangible presence of the Lord in my walk on a daily basis has made the difference between going through the motions, as opposed to experiencing an exciting adventure. Every day with the Lord is a day of discovery.

As we know, until the coming of the Son of God, the only nation with the knowledge of God was Israel. Jesus was a Jew, and He came first and foremost to the Jews. The Jews' belief that Jehovah was enshrined behind the curtain in the temple surely gave them an edge with their religious posture toward the other nations. After all, who else could make such a claim?

However, when Jesus died, the curtain that separated the holy place from the holy of holies was ripped from top to bottom. This supernatural event served as a public notice from God that He was "out and about." He now officially belongs to the entire world, and heaven will be populated with those from every tribe, tongue, nation, and people. "Ask of me, and I will make the nations your heritage, and the ends of the earth your possession" (Psalm 2:8 RSV).

He will live in the hearts of all people, and He will be their God. The day of a "smoldering national pride," whereby only one people hold the truth of God, is over. The anointing of the Holy Spirit has come, and He is filling the church worldwide.

2. Your latter shall be greater because: Our God is a God of increase, not a God of decrease (Genesis 1:28).

I mentioned earlier that the normal projection for God's people is increase. Jesus intended that His disciples would evangelize the entire world. There is no other way to interpret Matthew 28:16–20 or Revelation 5:9–10.

All of this is juxtaposed to a failing world system. Satan is the god of this world, and he is a loser. Everything else in the natural cycle decreases, runs down, or runs out. Man in his natural state is a user. He uses until there is no more. The end of the natural state is depletion; not so with God. Consider these:

- "Of the increase of his government and peace there will be no end" (Isaiah 9:7).
- "The LORD blessed the latter part of Job's life more than the first" (Job 42:12).
- Everyone who trusts in the Lord can claim this prayer: "May the LORD make you increase, both you and your children" (Psalm 115:14).
- "Jesus grew in wisdom and stature and in favor with God and men" (Luke 2:52).
- John the Baptist said: "He must become greater; I must become less" (John 3:30).
- "Hear, O Israel, and be careful to obey so that it may go well with you and that you may increase greatly" (Deuteronomy 6:3).
- "I will surely bless you and make your descendants as numerous as the stars in the sky and as the sand on the seashore" (Genesis 22:17).

He also said, "I am the Alpha and the Omega, the First and the Last, the Beginning and the End" (Revelation 22:13). Before you consider bemoaning and berating your earthly circumstance, consider your God. The Lord is about the restoration of all things, and you and I are included. Selah!

3. Your latter shall be greater because: He said so! (Psalm 138:2b).

Why can we not accept God's Word as the final authority in our lives? Are we the only generation from whom He has required this? Whether we are seeing things with our eyes or not, the truth is established and we can stand on the eternal Word of God (Ephesians 6:10). The church needs to return to a "persistent confidence" in God's Word.

As we move into the murky, chaotic future, the tribulation that is coming upon the world will elicit a confidence crisis throughout the culture. In tandem with this loss of confidence, the church will step into the gap to provide a helping hand to those ill-prepared. As God brings distraught, dysfunctional people to our doorstep, we will direct them to the source—Jesus Christ—and the life that flows from knowing Him.

Having lived on both sides of the equation—the redeemed as well as the unredeemed world—the Christian, empowered by the Holy Spirit, can, by the grace of God, point others to "the faith that was once delivered to the saints." Why will all this be necessary?

We in the Western world are surrounded by cultural atheism—saturated to the point that we no longer know right from wrong. Think of it this way. A fish has no concept of what it means to be wet. Why? Because it has never experienced being dry. In a similar way, the culture has saturated many Americans with sin to the point that they no longer can discern righteousness. However, God's Word is still true, and sin is still sin, according to the Word of God. If we relinquish the Word, we are slaves to the suffocating godless culture, and the kingdom of God is compromised.

What is needed is for the leadership of the church to return to a rock-solid confidence in the Word of God. People want to know there is a sure Word of God in troubled times. Friends, these are troubled times. There is a thin veil of civility that covers our day-to-day living, but it remains ever so fragile. When stressed, the veil can quickly come down, and that which lurks behind the veil is frightening.

The churches that are alive today are churches engulfed by Fire and yoked to the Word of God. Thank God for a clear Word in an unclear world! The great German philosopher Immanuel Kant, who possessed one of the best minds of modern times, said, "The existence of the Bible is the greatest blessing which humanity ever experienced."[146] If we want folks to come to faith, we must preach the Bible. "Faith comes from hearing he message, and the message is heard through the word of Christ" (Romans 10:17).

4. Your latter shall be greater because: The future belongs to God's people (Acts 1:8; 3:21).

History is moving toward a destiny, a prophetic gathering point, where all things—things in heaven and things on earth—will bow and acknowledge the Lord Jesus Christ (Romans 8:22; Revelation 21:1–5). With this calendar event, the earth will be renewed and restored to a paradisiacal existence so that the cosmos and created order will again reflect the Creator's original intention. I want to be a part of this restoration . . . how about you?

Before this restoration takes place, we the church are empowered by the Spirit to unveil the kingdom of Christ to the peoples of the world in advance of its apocalyptic climax. The end times church is to be seen as:

- An advance team for the soon and coming King
- An outpost for the New Jerusalem
- A microcosm for what God intends for all
- A prototype of the eternal age to come
- A basis of operation by which Christ's future reign can involve the present

The church is a future-oriented people to the core. Author John Mason says, "Those who predominantly talk about the past are going backward. Those who talk about the present are just maintaining. But those who talk about the future are growing." The plain fact is, "You can't walk backward into the future." And "don't let your past mistakes become memorials. They should be cremated, not embalmed."[147]

For the Christian believer, the future holds only promise and a life of joy in the presence of the Lord. You just cannot lose with God. Listen to the Apostle Paul: "For this slight momentary affliction is preparing for us an eternal weight of glory beyond all comparison because we look not to the things that are seen, but to the things that are unseen" (2 Corinthians 4:17–18 RSV).

5. Your latter shall be greater because: Hope is our hallmark (Colossians 1:27; 1 Timothy 1:1).

On New Year's Eve, 1999, Pope John Paul II challenged the pilgrims in St. Peter's Square to enter the 21st century determined to conquer fear and "rediscover the Spirit of Hope." The same night in Times Square, crowds watched the Millennium ball made of Waterford crystal (dubbed the "Star of Hope") drop during the last minute, prior to singing "Auld Lang Syne."

All things considered, life's priorities are determined mostly by what lies ahead. There is a predisposition in human nature that demands we anticipate something better to come. Victor Frankel, in *Man's Search for Meaning*, said the thing that made the difference between those who survived the Holocaust and those who perished, in many cases, was the degree of hope they nourished.

Last year I watched a TV special titled *C. S. Lewis vs. Sigmund Freud*. Both men were brilliant individuals who left a mark on their generation. However, Lewis died in the faith, an encouraged man. Freud died distraught and discouraged, "having no hope and without God in the world." (Ephesians 2:12 RSV)

The Bible tells us the human race is depraved at heart, corrupt of affection, self-seeking in relationships, fearful of death, enslaved to forces of darkness, and candidates for everlasting wrath. Into this picture steps Jesus Christ to bring good news. He alone has taken away the reproach of sin, and bids us, in the Sermon on the Mount, to come and live with Him. The time is short. We must reach the peoples of the earth with His message of hope.

Do you realize that 67 percent of all humans, from AD 30 to the present, have never heard the name of Jesus? Further, there are more unevangelized people in our world right now, than the number of times an average heart beats from the day of birth to age 75.[148]

Now is the time to shine. God is calling the church to a new dimension of faith in these latter days. Recently, the much-anointed vocal group, Higher Ground, released a new song during a ministry weekend at our church. The words of this song enshrine, I believe, the new dimension of faith which the church is being summoned to at this hour of history. Listen with your spirit to the words:

> There are men of faith and vision
> Seeing brighter every day,
> Men of Godly wisdom
> Transcending their own day.
> Beyond the veil of limitation,
> They have risen by degree
> To a higher place established
> By the words of their decree.
> Who will fulfill his purpose—
> Enter in on this Third Day?
> There's a company that's going,
> Those who will transcend the day.
> There's a place prepared and waiting,
> To be claimed and occupied.
> There's a day quickly breaking;
> See the light across the sky.
> Some see past the darkness,
> As the dawn is bringing light
> Through the door; the rays are shining,
> Healing all who are in sight.
> Who will dare to follow
> And transcend the days?
> Who, like Paul and David,
> Will unlock the way?
> To a place prepared and waiting,
> To be claimed and occupied –
> There's a day quickly breaking;
> See the light across the sky.[149]

6. Your latter shall be greater because: There is more! (Jeremiah 33:3; Isaiah 48:6)

Before Christopher Columbus set sail from Spain in 1492, his country's national motto was "Ne Plus Ultra," meaning *There is nothing beyond*. In its own estimation, Spain occupied the very ends of the earth. Geographically speaking, Spain was as far as any traveler would ever dare to go.

However, "After the explorer returned with glowing reports of bountiful lands, the motto was revised to 'Plus Ultra,' meaning *There is something beyond*."[150]

The believer in Christ is a "Plus Ultra" person. Conversion turns sinners into "round-earthers." Sometimes the church just needs to be reevangelized and reconverted to the great mandate of Christ. We are destined to be hope-filled witnesses to the King of Glory, for we have not yet begun to see the full glory, mercy, and greatness of God.

As you consider ministry in the 21st century, know that the God who brought the Lord Jesus Christ from death to life again, will empower you anew to be both successful and faithful in all He has called you to do. Each Sunday as we worship the Lord in our sanctuary, we face bold gold letters attached to the back wall of the platform. The words are from 1 Chronicles 29:11. I leave you with these words as an exclamation for the future:

Yours, O LORD, is the greatness and the power and the glory and the majesty and the splendor, for everything in heaven and earth is yours. Yours, O LORD, is the kingdom; you are exalted as head over all.

Endnotes

1. *The Works of John Wesley*, 3rd ed. (Grand Rapids, MI: Baker Book House, 1978), 1:103.

2. John Wesley, *Journal* (15 March 1739): 176.

3. Ibid.

4. Ibid.

5. John Wesley, *Journal* (29 March 1739): 185.

6. John Wesley, *Journal* (2 April 1739): 185.

7. J. I. Packer, Merrill C. Tenney, and William White, Jr., *The Bible Almanac: A Comprehensive Handbook of the People of the Bible and How They Lived* (Nashville: Thomas Nelson Publishers, 1980), 692.

8. William Sanford LaSor, *Great Personalities of the Old Testament: Their Lives and Times* (Grand Rapids, MI: Revell, 1959), 130.

9. Vinson Synan, "Jihad vs. The Great Commission" (lecture, Charismatic Leaders Fellowship, Jacksonville, FL, January 2005).

10. Harvey Cox, *Fire From Heaven: The Rise of Pentecostal Spirituality and the Reshaping of Religion in the 21st Century* (Upper Saddle River, NJ: Addison-Wesley Publishing Company, 1995), xv.

11. Scott McDermott, e-mail message to author, March 25, 2005.

12. "Act of Humility Sparks Awakening In Texas," Charisma Now Internet News, November 27, 2000.

13. Wesley Duewel, *Revival Fire* (Grand Rapids, MI: Zondervan, 1995), 128–129.

14. Mario Murillo, *Fresh Fire* (Port Bolivar, TX: Anthony Douglas Publishing, 1991), 129.

15. Ibid.

16. *Smith Wigglesworth on Spirit Filled Living* (New Kensington, PA: Whitaker House, 1998), 119.

17. Michael Slaughter, *Spiritual Entrepreneurs: 6 Principles for Risking Renewal* (Nashville: Abingdon, 1995), 19.

18. Robert C. Girard, *Brethren, Hang Loose* (Grand Rapids, MI: Zondervan, 1973), 68.

19. Bill Gothard, "Understanding the Fear of the Lord" (lecture, Pastors Seminar, Dayton, Ohio, 1982).

20. *Webster's New World Dictionary of the American Language*, s.v. "Catalysis."

21. Bob George, *Classic Christianity: Life's Too Short to Miss the Real Thing* (Eugene, OR: Harvest House, 1989), 47.

22. C. Peter Wagner, *The New Apostolic Churches* (Ventura, CA: Regal, 1998), 14.

23. Peter Hocken, *The Glory and the Shame* (Macomb, IL: Eagle Publications, 1994), 65.

24. Patrick Johnstone and Jason Mandryk, *Operation World: When We Pray God Works*, 21st Century ed. (Carlisle, Cumbria, UK: Paternoster Lifestyle, 2001), 755.

25. Francis MacNutt, *The Nearly Perfect Crime: How the Church Almost Killed the Ministry of Healing* (Grand Rapids, MI: Chosen Books, 2005), 212.

26. Vinson Synan, *The Century of the Holy Spirit: 100 Years of Pentecostal and Charismatic Renewal* (Nashville: Thomas Nelson, 2001), ix.

27. Ibid., x.

28. *A Journey Beyond: The Autobiography of G. Ross Freeman* (Franklin, TN: Providence House Publishers, 2001), 2–3.

29. William P. Wilson and Ross Whetstone, "A Brief History of the UMRSF" (computer printout, 1994), 2–3.

30. Ibid., 4.

31. Ibid., 5.

32. "One Church's Pentecost" *Ministries Today*, September/October 1992, 21–22.

33. Ibid., 22.

34. Ibid.

35. Bruce Shelley, *Christian History in Plain Language* (Nashville: Thomas Nelson, 1995), 3.

36. J. I. Packer, *Knowing God* (Downers Grove, IL: InterVarsity Press, 1973), 171.

37. John R. W. Stott, *The Cross of Christ* (Downers Grove, IL: Inter-Varsity Press, 1986), 190.

38. Ibid., 170.

39. Leon Morris, *The Cross of Christ* (Grand Rapids, MI: William B. Erdmans Publishing, 1965), 159.

40. John Wesley, *Journal* (24 May 1738): 103

41. Ibid., (28 March 1738): 86

42. Ellen Logan Morris, "The Transforming Life" (DMin diss., Ashland Theological Seminary), 135–136.

43. Colleen Carroll, *The New Faithful: Why Young Adults are Embracing Christian Orthodoxy* (Chicago: Loyola Press, 2002), 15–16.

44. John R. W. Stott, *The Cross of Christ* (Downers Grove: Inter-Varsity Press, 1986), 19–20.

45. Ibid., 21.

46. Dallas Willard, *The Divine Conspiracy: Rediscovering Our Hidden Life in God* (New York: Harper, 1997), 2.

47. Francis MacNutt, "A Near-Death Experience," *The Healing Line/Newsletter*, January/February 2005, 1.

48. Ramsay MacMullen, *Christianizing the Roman Empire: A.D. 100–400* (New Haven, CT: Yale University Press, 1984), 66.

49. *Randy Clark School of Healing and Impartation Manual* (Mechanicsburg, PA: Global Awakening, 2005), 6.

50. Francis MacNutt, "A Near-Death Experience," *The Healing Line/Newsletter*, January/February 2005, 1.

51. Francis MacNutt, *The Nearly Perfect Crime: How the Church Almost Killed the Ministry of Healing* (Grand Rapids, MI: Chosen Books, 2005), 146.

52. Ibid.

53. Bill Jackson, *The Quest for the Radical Middle* (Cape Town, South Africa: Vineyard International Publishing, 1999), 121.

54. Charles H. Kraft, *Confronting Powerless Christianity: Evangelicals and the Missing Dimension* (Grand Rapids, MI: Chosen Books, 2002), 7.

55. Charles H. Kraft, *I Give You Authority* (Grand Rapids, MI: Chosen Books, 1997), 13.

56. Charles H. Kraft, *Confronting Powerless Christianity: Evangelicals and the Missing Dimension* (Grand Rapids, MI: Chosen Books, 2002), 7–8.

57. *Randy Clark School of Healing and Impartation Manual* (Mechanicsburg, PA: Global Awakening, 2005), 119.

58. Ibid.

59. Ibid., 120.

60. Frank Damazio, *Seasons of Revival: Understanding the Appointed Times of Spiritual Refreshing* (Portland, OR: City Christian Publishing, 1996), 242.

61. Carlos Annacondia, *Listen to Me Satan!: Exercising Authority Over the Devil in Jesus' Name* (Lake Mary, FL: Creation House, 1998), 154.

62. Dennis Bennett and Rita Bennett, *The Holy Spirit and You: A Guide to the Spirit-Filled Life* (Orlando, FL: Bridge-Logos Publishers, 1971), 113–114.

63. Vinson Synan, *In the Latter Days: The Outpouring of the Holy Spirit in the Twentieth Century*, rev. ed. (Longwood, FL: Xulon Press, 2001), 4.

64. Francis MacNutt, *The Nearly Perfect Crime: How the Church Almost Killed the Ministry of Healing* (Grand Rapids, MI: Chosen Books, 2005), 213.

65. Gregory A. Boyd, *God at War: The Bible & Spiritual Conflict* (Downers Grove, IL: InterVarsity Press, 1997), 11.

66. Ibid., 17.

67. Ibid.

68. Gregory A Boyd, *Satan and The Problem of Evil* (Downers Grove, IL: InterVarsity Press, 2001, 35.

69. Ibid., 255.

70. Doug Bandow and David L. Schindler, *Wealth, Poverty, and Human Destiny* (Wilmington, DE: ISI Books, 2003), 321.

71. James Luther Mays, *Amos: A Commentary*, The Old Testament Library (Philadelphia: Westminster Press, 1969), 5.

72. Doug Stringer, *Passion for God, Compassion for Souls* (Muncie, IN: Prayer Point Press, 2001), 111.

73. James Robison, *The Absolutes* (Carol Stream, IL: Tyndale, 2002), 195.

74. Ibid., 206.

75. "Oil Discovery Paying Off For Church", *This Week* in Pickering-ton, OH, June 2, 1997.

76. Niagara Falls Hotels, Tours, and Attractions, "Facts about Niagara Falls," *Niagara Falls Live*, http://www.niagarafallslive.com/Facts_about_Niagara_Falls.htm (accessed May 18, 2006).

77. J. David Hoke, "Isn't Being Good Good Enough?" *New Horizons Community Church*, www.horizonsnet.org/sermons/oc04.html (accessed May 18, 2006).

78. Francis Fukuyama, *The Great Disruption: Human Nature and the Reconstitution of Social Order* (New York: Free Press, 1999), 13–14.

79. Charles Colson, *Kingdoms in Conflict* (Grand Rapids, MI: Morrow/Zondervan, 1987), 225.

80. Robert Bork, *Slouching Towards Gomorrah: Modern Liberalism and American Decline* (New York: HarperCollins Publishers, 1996), 157.

81. Stephen L. Carter, *The Culture of Disbelief* (New York: Basic Books, 1993), 173.

82. Lyle E. Schaller, *Discontinuity and Hope: Radical Change and the Path to the Future* (Nashville: Abingdon Press, 1999), 167.

83. Ibid., 215.

84. Robert Bork, *Slouching Towards Gomorrah: Modern Liberalism and American Decline* (New York: HarperCollins Publishers, 1996), 127, 138.

85. Richard John Neuhaus, "Scandal Time," *First Things*, http://www.firstthings.com/ftissues/ft0206/public.html (accessed May 18, 2006).

86. "The Moral Homefront," *Christianity Today*, October 2004, 152.

87. Samuel P. Huntington, *The Clash of Civilizations and the Remaking of World Order* (New York: Simon & Schuster, 1996), 28.

88. Ibid., 47.

89. Charles Krauthammer, "This war is also about — deeply about — sex," *Jewish World Review*, May 7, 2004. Online at http://www.jewishworldreview.com/cols/krauthammer050704.asp. Accessed May 19, 2006.

90. Robert Bork, *Slouching Towards Gomorrah: Modern Liberalism and American Decline* (New York: HarperCollins Publishers, 1996), 336.

91. Os Guinness, *Prophetic Untimeliness: A Challenge to the Idol of Relevance* (Grand Rapids, MI: Baker Books, 2003), 71.

92. Graham Johnston, *Preaching to a Postmodern World: A Guide to Reaching Twenty-First Century Listeners* (Grand Rapids, MI: Baker Books, 2001), 97.

93. Wade Clark Roof, *Spiritual Marketplace: Baby Boomers and the Remaking of American Religion* (Princeton: Princeton, 1999), 84.

94. Barna Research Group Ltd., Oxnard, CA. "Examples of Similarities of Behavior Between Christians and Non-Christians." *The Barna Report*, 1997.

95. Ron Sider, interview by Stan Guthrie, *Christianity Today*, April 2005, 70.

96. Stephen L. Carter, *Integrity* (New York: Basic Books, 1996), 29.

97. George Barna, *Think Like Jesus: Make the Right Decision Every Time* (Hillsborough, NC: Issachar, 2003), 16.

98. Ibid., 22.

99. Ron Sider, interview by Stan Guthrie, *Christianity Today*, April 2005, 71.

100. Harold A. Netland, *Encountering Religious Pluralism: The Challenge to Christian Faith and Mission* (Downers Grove, IL: InterVarsity Press, 2001), 59.

101. Ibid., 68.

102. Os Guinness, *Prophetic Untimeliness: A Challenge to the Idol of Relevance* (Grand Rapids, MI: Baker Books, 2003), 11.

103. Ibid., 12.

104. James Woolsey, interview with Sean Hannity, *Hannity and Colmes.* Fox News Channel, January 30, 2005.

105. George Otis, Jr., *God's Trademarks: How to Determine Whether a Message, Ministry, or Strategy Is Truly from God* (Grand Rapids, MI: Chosen Books, 2000), 137.

106. Ibid., 138.

107. Ibid., 139.

108. Os Guinness, *Prophetic Untimeliness: A Challenge to the Idol of Relevance* (Grand Rapids, MI: Baker Books, 2003), 78.

109. Rabbi Daniel Lapin, "Watchman On the Wall: Washington Briefing on Marriage and the Family," (lecture, National Pastors Briefing, Washington, DC, May 2004).

110. Tommy Tenney, *The God Chasers: My Soul Follows Hard After Thee* (Shippensburg, PA: Destiny Image Publishers, Inc., 1998), Introduction, 1.

111. Eddie L. Hyatt, *2000 Years of Charismatic Christianity: A 21st Century Look at Church History from a Pentecostal/Charismatic Perspective* (Tulsa, OK: Hyatt International Ministries, Inc., 1996), 150.

112. Ibid.

113. Ibid., 151.

114. Ibid.

115. Ibid., 156.

116. Vinson Synan, *The Century of the Holy Spirit: 100 Years of Pentecostal and Charismatic Renewal* (Nashville: Thomas Nelson, 2001), 47.

117. Ibid., 49.

118. Eddie L. Hyatt, *2000 Years of Charismatic Christianity: A 21st Century Look at Church History from a Pentecostal/Charismatic Perspective* (Tulsa, OK: Hyatt International Ministries, Inc., 1996), 157.

119. Geoff Waugh, *Flashpoints of Revival: History's Mighty Revivals* (Phoenix, AZ: Revival Press, 1998), 33.

120. Ibid., 34.

121. Wesley Duewel, *Revival Fire* (Grand Rapids, MI: Zondervan, 1995), 186.

122. Winkie Pratney, *Revival: Principles to Change the World* (New Kensington, PA: Whitaker House, 1983), 160.

123. Eddie L. Hyatt, *2000 Years of Charismatic Christianity: A 21st Century Look at Church History from a Pentecostal/Charismatic Perspective* (Tulsa, OK: Hyatt International Ministries, Inc., 1996), 185.

124. Ibid., 195.

125. Ibid., 196.

126. Vinson Synan, *The Century of the Holy Spirit: 100 Years of Pentecostal and Charismatic Renewal* (Nashville: Thomas Nelson, 2001), 109.

127. Ibid., 111.

128. Mark A. Noll, *Turning Points: Decisive Moments in the History of Christianity* (Grand Rapids, MI: Baker Books, 1997), 299.

129. Nicholas D. Kristof, "Christianity Marching Up Tough Roads in Africa, Asia," *Columbus Dispatch*, March 29, 2005.

130. Mike Bickle, *Passion for Jesus: Perfecting Extravagant Love for God* (Lake Mary, FL: Creation House Publishers, 1993), 197.

131. Wolfgang Simpson, *Houses that Change the World: The Return of the House Churches* (Carlisle, Cumbria, UK: OM Publishing, 1998), 47.

132. Ibid., 49.

133. Ibid., 50.

134. Ibid., 51.

135. Robert E. Weber, *Ancient-Future Faith: Rethinking Evangelicalism for a Postmodern World*, (Grand Rapids, MI: Baker Books, 1999), 72.

136. Wolfgang Simpson, *Houses that Change the World: The Return of the House Churches* (Carlisle, Cumbria, UK: OM Publishing, 1998), 52.

137. "Transformation in Congregations: Introduction," in *Hope For Your Future: Theological Voices from the Pastorate*, William H. Lazareth, ed. (Grand Rapids, MI: William B. Erdmans Publishing, 2002), 165.

138. Philip Jenkins, *The Next Christendom: The Coming of Global Christianity* (Oxford: Oxford University Press, 2002), 215.

139. C. Peter Wagner, *ChurchQuake: The Explosive Dynamics of the New Apostolic Revolution* (Ventura, CA: Regal Books, 1999), 5.

140. Ibid., 19.

141. Alister E. McGrath, *The Future of Christianity*, Blackwell Manifestos (City: Blackwell Publishers, 2002), 99.

142. Ibid., 100.

143. Norman Podhoretz, *The Prophets: Who They Were, What They Are* (New York: Free Press, 2002), 289.

144. Executive Editor, Gregory A. Lent, *The Complete Biblical Library: The Old Testament* (Springfield, MO: World Library Press, 1999), 15:525.

145. *Harper Study Bible* (Grand Rapids, MI: Zondervan Publishing, 1971), 1405.

146. Reinhard Bonnke, *Evangelism by Fire: Igniting Your Passion for the Lost* (Waco, TX: Word Publishing, 1990), 75.

147. John Mason, *You're Born an Original, Don't Die a Copy!* (Tulsa, OK: Insight International, 1993), 39.

148. Don Richardson, "Perspectives on World Missions Course," *Unleashing the Gospel* (Columbus, Ohio: Lecture, March 5, 2002, Cooper Road Vineyard Church of Columbus).

149. Higher Ground. "See the Light Across the Sky," (Nashville: SpiritGate Music/SongChannel Music, 2005).

150. David Bryant, *Christ Is All! A Joyful Manifesto on the Supremacy of God's Son* (New Providence, NJ: New Providence Publishers, 2004), 235.

For more information
or to contact Pastor Scott T. Kelso,
please visit

www.TrinityFLC.org